Words to Live By

With Gratitude
Ann,
For being an
encouraging Presence
full of light and
love!

♡ Celene Ibrahim

Thanks for
all the BFI
support!

[signature]

WORDS TO LIVE BY

Sacred Sources for Interreligious Engagement

EDITED BY OR N. ROSE,
HOMAYRA ZIAD, AND SOREN M. HESSLER

ORBIS BOOKS

Maryknoll, New York 10545

ORBIS BOOKS
Maryknoll, New York 10545

Fathers and Brothers
MARYKNOLL™

Founded in 1970, Orbis Books endeavors to publish works that enlighten the mind, nourish the spirit, and challenge the conscience. The publishing arm of the Maryknoll Fathers and Brothers, Orbis seeks to explore the global dimensions of the Christian faith and mission, to invite dialogue with diverse cultures and religious traditions, and to serve the cause of reconciliation and peace. The books published reflect the views of their authors and do not represent the official position of the Maryknoll Society. To learn more about Maryknoll and Orbis Books, please visit our website at www.maryknollsociety.org.

Library of Congress Cataloging-in-Publication Data

Names: Rose, Or N., editor.
Title: Words to live by : sacred sources of interreligious engagement / Or N. Rose, Homayra Ziad, and Soren M. Hessler, editors.
Description: Maryknoll : Orbis Books, 2018. | Includes bibliographical references and index.
Identifiers: LCCN 2017058670 (print) | LCCN 2018006557 (ebook) | ISBN 9781608337453 (e-book) | ISBN 9781626982796 (pbk.)
Subjects: LCSH: Conduct of life. | Religions. | Religious ethics.
Classification: LCC BJ1595 (ebook) | LCC BJ1595 .W795 2018 (print) | DDC 201/.5—dc23
LC record available at https://lccn.loc.gov/2017058670

"Blessed be the covenant of love
between the hidden and the revealed."

—Leonard Cohen, *Book of Mercy, #14*

We lovingly dedicate this volume to our spouses:

Judith Rosenbaum
Ali Tajdar
Jennifer Quigley

For Ann,

Thank you for your
ongoing collaboration.

Blessings,

Contents

Foreword by Dr. Francis X. Clooney, SJ   *xi*

Acknowledgments   *xiii*

Introduction   *xv*

I

TEXTUAL REFLECTIONS ON PARTICULARISM AND UNIVERSALISM

1. Judith Simmer-Brown, *Negotiating Conflicting
   Religious Claims through Inquiry:* The Kalama Sutta   *3*

2. Anantanand Rambachan, *Are Religious Differences
   Only Semantic?*   *13*

3. Mahan Mirza, *Balancing Theological Exclusivism
   with Metaphysical Inclusivism*   *23*

4. Abigail Clauhs, *"The Cathedral of the World":
   Interconnection in Difference*   *31*

5. Amos Yong and Timothy T. N. Lim, *Acts 2 and
   Interreligious Engagement: Pentecostal and
   Evangelical Reflections*   *42*

6. Nancy Fuchs Kreimer, *Wrestling with Chosenness:
   A Personal Reflection*   *53*

II

PERSONAL VIRTUES IN SUPPORT OF INTERRELIGIOUS ENGAGEMENT

7. Burton L. Visotzky, *"Be as Gentle as the Reed":*
   A Rabbinic Tale about Confronting the Other   *65*

8. Jennifer Howe Peace, *"Just as I Have Loved You":*
   A Christian Hermeneutic of Love
   as a Resource for Interfaith Engagement   *72*

9. Celene Ibrahim, Sūrah al-'Alaq *and*
   Dispositions for Interreligious Engagement   *82*

10. Esther Boyd, *Hospitality, Communal Responsibility,*
    and Humility: Secular Humanism
    and "The New Colossus"   *93*

III

SACRED PRACTICES AND INTERRELIGIOUS COMMITMENTS

11. Homayra Ziad, *Meeting in the Realm of Poetry*
    and Music: Qawwali *Devotional Music*   *103*

12. Varun Soni, *"On the Rosary of My Breath":*
    Nusrat Fateh Ali Khan's Mystical Fusion   *112*

13. Joshua M. Z. Stanton, *Sacred Debate:*
    Makhloket and Interreligious Dialogue   *121*

14. Andrew R. Davis, *Biblical Exegesis as*
    Interreligious Dialogue and Spiritual Practice   *129*

15. Sherman A. Jackson, *"And Among the People*
    of the Book...": Reading beyond Offense,
    Confirmation, or Gratification   *139*

16. Simran Jeet Singh, *Unity and Multiplicity:*
    The Practice of Sohila and Sikh Theology   *148*

IV

INTERRELIGIOUS ENGAGEMENT AND THE PUBLIC SQUARE

17. Hussein Rashid, *Opening the Door: Imam Ali and*
    New Conversations in Interreligious Dialogue   *159*

18. Jeffery D. Long, *Swami Vivekananda's Address*
    to the First Parliament of the World's Religions
    on September 11, 1893   *170*

19. Ruben L. F. Habito, Nostra Aetate*: Catholic Charter*
    for Interreligious Engagement   *180*

20. Rahuldeep Gill, *"Whatever Pleases the One":*
    Guru Nanak's Response to Violence and Warfare   *191*

21. Or N. Rose, *Spiritual Activism:*
    Abraham Joshua Heschel's Telegram
    to President Kennedy   *200*

22. MT Dávila, *Archbishop Oscar Romero's*
    Call for Peace and Reconciliation   *209*

23. Amy Eilberg, *Clergy Beyond Borders:*
    A Caravan of Reconciliation   *219*

Afterword: A Note on Interreligious Learning
    by Rabbi Daniel Lehmann and
    Rev. Dr. Mary Elizabeth Moore   *229*

Contributors   *231*

Index   *243*

Foreword

In September 2015 Pope Francis spoke in the September 11 Memorial Museum in Manhattan, addressing a gathering of about four hundred religious leaders and scholars from many faith traditions. I was privileged to be present that day, and to hear the Pope's impassioned plea that religious people of all faith traditions work together to give a counter-witness to fanaticism and violence perpetrated in the name of religion: "I trust that our presence together will be a powerful sign of our shared desire to be a force for reconciliation, peace and justice in this community and throughout the world. For all our differences and disagreements, we can experience a world of peace. In opposing every attempt to create a rigid uniformity, we can and must build unity on the basis of our diversity of languages, cultures and religions, and lift our voices against everything which would stand in the way of such unity. Together we are called to say 'no' to every attempt to impose uniformity and 'yes' to a diversity accepted and reconciled."

In hearing such words, we will first think of action for peace, work together in facing today's problems. And so it should be. But such work is not done quickly, as if started today, finished tomorrow—or next year, or ten years from now. Community in solidarity needs to be a way of life, for a lifetime. For this, we need to grow deep roots, nourished by wisdom that endures. We need to keep returning, with humility and patience, to the sources that have given faith the strength to do the needful for centuries and millennia, treasures that once more today can light our paths in the gloom enveloping us.

Words to Live By: Sacred Sources for Interreligious Engagement is a precious gift for this longer journey and deeper quest. More than twenty personal reflections on the holy sources testify to the truth and strength and life arising from these wellsprings, and at the same time make those resources more readily available—to be glimpsed, heard, savored, and enjoyed—in a small and compact volume, itself a harmony of voices now heard together. These testimonies invite us to go deeper into traditions we know well, and also to visit other traditions perhaps for the first time, and find nourishment there, too.

Readers can all be grateful to Or Rose, Homayra Ziad, and Soren Hessler for working together on this volume, allowing contributors to speak to the same heart of the matter, yet from four vantage points: textual reflection, personal virtue, sacred practice, interreligious engagement in the public square. We need them all, and all of them together. And so it is that we can open this book wherever we wish, but in the end we keep finding our way back to that unity in diversity to which Pope Francis and other wise leaders call us, every "no" gently but firmly turned into a "yes" to peace and justice and love upon this earth.

Francis X. Clooney, SJ
Parkman Professor of Divinity
Harvard University

Acknowledgments

We wish to thank the following individuals and institutions for their support of this project:

Robert Ellsberg
Dr. Jennifer Howe Peace
Rabbi Sharon Cohen Anisfeld
Marilyn Stern

Hebrew College
Boston University School of Theology

Special thanks to Dr. Francis X. Clooney, SJ,
for writing the foreword to this volume
and to Rabbi Daniel Lehmann
and Rev. Dr. Mary Elizabeth Moore
for writing the afterword.

Introduction

In a rapidly shrinking and interconnected world, in which people of different beliefs and commitments are interacting in unprecedented ways, can religion be a force for good? Advances in high-speed communication and travel, along with increased migration and urbanization, have triggered unexpected encounters among people from diverse religious traditions. The ubiquity of media has brought the stories of various faith communities to the attention of people around the globe. More than ever, we need a robust set of intellectual, spiritual, and ethical resources to help us engage constructively across lines of religious and cultural difference. In fashioning an interreligious ethos appropriate for the current age, we must draw on the best of our traditions to meet the unique challenges and opportunities of this era. Which poetic, prophetic, liturgical, or legal teachings might help us attend thoughtfully to our similarities and differences as adherents of particular faith traditions and as members of a common human family? Which interpretive approaches—old and new—might we utilize to do the textual work creatively and responsibly?

This anthology is but one attempt to respond to what is a critical need. We have invited a diverse group of scholars, educators, public intellectuals, and activists from across the United States to share materials that they have found valuable in their work as interreligious bridge-builders. In issuing this call, we asked participants not only to choose a relevant text, but to share with readers its historical and literary contexts, and to explain how it inspires, guides, or authorizes their work in the interreligious sphere. We also asked each writer to provide a series of guiding questions for reflection and discussion, as well as suggestions for further reading.

Not only do the contributors to this collection come from different religions, they are also involved in different forms of interreligious engagement: dialogue, study, activism, contemplative practice, and human development. This is reflected in the foci and style of the contributions. Further, our writers hold diverse theological, social, and political views; some identify as progressive, moderate, or conservative, while others eschew these categories. These differences in belief and opinion exist both within and across the religious traditions represented in this volume. However, all of the writers believe that there are textual resources in their respective heritages that can help people connect constructively across religious lines and reflect on the spiritual and ethical significance of such encounters.

In shaping this anthology, we grouped the individual chapters into four broad sections, each with a different thematic focus:

1. textual reflections on particularism and universalism

2. personal virtues in support of interreligious engagement

3. sacred practices and interreligious commitments

4. interreligious engagement and the public square

We chose these categories to help the reader explore different types of interreligious activity. However, these are not strict divisions, as some contributions could be placed in more than one section of the book. We encourage you to make creative use of this collection, allowing your interests and curiosity to guide your reading experience.

As editors, we also recognize that there are teachings in our respective traditions that speak disparagingly about people from other religious traditions and that are not particularly helpful in developing respectful interreligious relations. These texts must be explored critically, as they can be too easily deployed to legitimate chauvinistic attitudes and destructive behaviors. In fact, many of the writers in this volume do exactly this type of interpretive work daily in their teaching, preaching, counseling, organizing, and writing. However, that is not the primary focus of this collection, which aims to lift up positive resources for engagement and reflection. Within this framework, however, some of our writers chose texts that contain challenging or troubling elements (sometimes interwoven with the constructive materials they wish to highlight) and/or that have been interpreted in insensitive and harmful ways by previous commentators.

It is important to add that, in conceiving of this collection, we were motivated both by negative and positive factors. That is to say, it is not only because of the existence of religious prejudice and violence that a volume like this is worthwhile; we also believe that interreligious study can help people of many walks of life reflect more deeply on their beliefs and practices, hone their core existential questions, and gain insight into the human condition. We can each personally attest to the transformative power of reading an illuminating or stirring teaching from another religious tradition and of studying with impassioned and open-hearted interlocutors from different faith communities. This book arises, in part, from the many positive experiences we have had engaging in and facilitating interreligious courses, workshops, and study groups.

As you read the materials in this anthology, we invite you to think about the sources that inform your own interfaith values and commitments. To what extent do you turn to religious (and/or secular) texts in considering your relationships with the religious other? Are there sources that you consider authoritative or particularly important in this context? If you identify with one (or more) of the traditions represented in this volume, how do you feel about the textual selections and reflections we have included? If you were asked to select one text from your religious tradition for an anthology like this (or for a class or discussion group), what would it be? What does it feel like to engage with writers from other religions on this topic? Do you find any of these sources or commentaries particularly compelling? Do you find any of them challenging or disquieting? If so, why?

It is our hope that this collection of primary sources and contemporary interpretations will serve to stimulate both your heart and mind, moving you to explore further the ideas and practices of other spiritual and ethical traditions and to engage meaningfully with people from different religious communities.

—Or N. Rose, Homayra Ziad, Soren M. Hessler

I

Textual Reflections on Particularism and Universalism

1

Negotiating Conflicting Religious Claims through Inquiry

The Kalama Sutta

JUDITH SIMMER-BROWN

The earliest discourses of the historical Buddha, Siddhartha Gautama, recorded in the Pali canon of the Theravada school, provide a refreshing, earthy wisdom that invites the listener into inquiry rather than belief. The Buddha lived from 560 to 480 BCE at a time of great spiritual ferment in India, a time that generated a plethora of spiritual teachers and lineages such as Jainism, classical Yoga schools, and the great philosophic schools of what came to be known as Hinduism. The Buddha's discourses turned away from philosophical investigation and meditative calisthenics and emphasized direct investigation of personal experience through mindfulness and awareness meditation. He also advised those who were not his students about how to deal with conflicting religious claims so prevalent in his milieu.

Among the most famous of the Buddha's early teachings is the Discourse to the Kalamas (*Kalama Sutta*).[1] The Discourse was originally preserved through memorization and eventually,

---

1. Anguttara-nikaya I.188–93. The Pali canon was divided and organized by length, topic, and iteration of its contents, and was cataloged according to the volume and page of the original palm leaf inscriptions. Thanks to the centuries of Pali scholarship in the West, there are concordances that enable the reader to access specific pages of the text by reference to volume and palm leaf page, here signified by

five hundred years later, became a written text. The translation bears the signs of its oral source with the signature introduction, "Thus have I heard," signifying that the Buddha's famous cousin Ananda, his attendant and official memorizer, was present when the teaching was given. The text still employs the mnemonic device of repetition of stock phrases and long passages, giving it a charming but archaic flavor. Still, the freshness of perspective and the invitation for inquiry peeks through the repetitive passages.

The township of Kesaputta was obviously in a heavily traveled region of India frequented by religious visionaries of all kinds, each of whom proclaimed the merits of their own doctrines and truths while maligning those of others. Residents of the town, known as Kalamas, were bewildered by this, and did not know how to respond to these many conflicting religious claims. It is clear from the Discourse that they were not Buddhists, and they wondered if the Buddha were not just another such visionary.

Thus have I heard. At one time, the Exalted One was walking on tour in Kosala with a large contingent of *bhikkhus* [monks] and arrived at a town named Kesaputta . . . Then the Kalamas of Kesaputta approached the Exalted One . . . When he was seated to one side, one of the Kalamas of Kesaputta said this to the Exalted One:

"There are, sir, certain recluses and Brahmins who come to Kesaputta. They explain and proclaim only their own doctrines, while the doctrines of others they abuse, despise, treat with contempt, and condemn. Also, sir, there are other recluses and Brahmins who come to Kesa-

---

I.188–93. An excellent translation of the full Nikaya text of the Anguttara-nikaya is *The Numerical Discourses of the Buddha*, translated by Bhikkhu Bodhi (Boston: Wisdom Publications, 2012).

putta. These also explain and proclaim their own doctrines, while the doctrines of others they abuse, despise,
treat with contempt, and condemn. Sir, we are in doubt
and perplexity about this. Who among these honorable
recluses speaks the truth and who speaks what is false?"

The Exalted One replied:

"Indeed, it is proper to be in doubt, Kalamas, and to
be perplexed. When there is a doubtful situation, perplexity arises. In such cases, do not accept a thing by
recollection, by tradition, by mere report, because it is
based on the authority of scriptures, by mere logic or
inference, by reflection on conditions, because of
reflection on or fondness for a certain theory, because it
merely seems suitable, nor thinking, 'The religious wan-
derer is respected by us.'

"But when you know for yourselves: 'These things
are unwholesome, blameworthy, reproached by the
wise, when undertaken and performed lead to harm and
suffering'—these you should reject . . .

"What do you think, Kalamas? When greed (hatred,
delusion) arises within a person, is it to one's benefit or
to one's detriment?"

"To one's detriment, sir."

"So, Kalamas, does this greedy (hateful, deluded)
person, being overpowered by greed (hatred, delusion)
and having lost control over his mind, kill living beings,
take what is not given, go with another's wife, tell lies,
and encourage others to do the same, which things are
to his detriment and suffering for a long time?"

"Yes, sir . . ."

"Kalamas, when you know for yourselves: 'These
things are unwholesome, blameworthy, reproached by
the wise, when undertaken and performed lead to one's
detriment and suffering'—these you should reject . . .

"Kalamas, when you know for yourselves: 'These
things are wholesome, not blameworthy, commended

by the wise, when undertaken and performed lead to one's benefit and happiness'—you should live undertaking these things."[2]

The Discourse to the Kalamas (*Kalama Sutta*) has tremendous relevance today because of the multi-religious world in which we live. Its advice applies to two dimensions of our times: advice for how the citizen of an interreligious world might assess the contributions of religious others, and advice for how the spiritual seeker might navigate conflicting religious claims while trying to develop certainty in anything.

Daily we have contact with religious others, and technology gives us access with the click of a mouse to information about this diversity in every corner of the globe. Everywhere we turn, religions are proclaiming their own scriptures, practices, and doctrines as superior while denigrating the religious traditions, practices, and communities of others. This environment leads to the extremes of religious exclusivism, seeing religions as rivals locked in adversarial struggle on the one hand, or mere religious relativism on the other, with no sense of how these claims relate to cultivating one's life path. On the exclusivist extreme, we are witnessing the horrifying spectacle of mass murders of religious others perpetrated every day. On the relativist extreme, people shrug their shoulders, discount all religions as equally irrelevant, and turn the page. We desperately need interreligious literacy in order to appreciate the genuine contributions of religions while discerning the damaging or destructive aspects of extremism.

Seekers of all ages who yearn for a meaningful spiritual life and journey can become bewildered by the multiplicity of teach-

---

2. "Discourse to the Kalamas (Kalama Sutta)," Anguttara Nikaya I.188–90, in *Early Buddhist Discourses,* ed. and trans. by John J. Holder (Indianapolis: Hackett Publishing, 2006), 20–23.

ers, practices, and communities they encounter. They are asked by everyone to have faith or belief, but they have no idea how to begin. And when they dive in with precipitous faith, they may eventually suffer profound disillusionment that shakes the very foundation of their spiritual aspirations.

The Buddha's advice to the Kalamas from twenty-six hundred years ago seems relevant for today. He suggests that requiring unquestioning faith is not a good foundation for a spiritual life. There should be proper bases for religious belief in scriptures, teachers, and doctrines. These bases are not mere philosophic logic or on spiritual charisma that evokes an emotional response. Instead, the Buddha invites us to look at the practical and ethical results that come from applying a particular set of teachings to daily life in order to determine their moral efficacy. Here and elsewhere he includes the Buddhist teachings themselves among those to be so tested—they are not to be matters of blind faith.[3]

The Discourse teaches how to develop healthy inquiry in the face of conflicting religious claims. It advises seekers to be cautious about ten common pitfalls in religious belief.[4]

1. *Ma anussavena*—Don't accept doctrines just because they are ancient and have been retold for years.

2. *Ma paramparaya*—Don't believe because it is traditional to do so, following the crowd.

3. *Ma itikiraya*—Don't accept something merely because of its fame or renown.

3. Vimamsaka-sutta, Majjhima Nikaya I.318–20, *The Middle Length Discourses of the Buddha*, translated by Bhikkhu Nanamoli and Bhikkhu Bodhi (Boston: Wisdom Publications, 1995), 415–18.

4. Bhikkhu Buddhadasa, "Help! The Kalama Sutta, Help!" *Buddha-Dharma Buddhadasa Archives*, originally published in *Keys to Natural Truth*, http://www.suanmokkh.org/archive/arts/message/kalama1.htm (accessed April 19, 2015).

4. *Ma pitakasampadanena*—Don't follow a teaching just because it is scriptural.

5. *Ma takkahetu*—Don't believe a teaching just because it is logical.

6. *Ma nayahetu*—Don't hold a truth just because of impressive philosophical argument.

7. *Ma akaraparivitakkena*—Don't consider common sense alone to be sufficient reason to follow a teaching.

8. *Ma ditthinijjhanakkhantiya*—Don't agree with something just because it seems to fit your already accepted ideas.

9. *Ma bhabbarupataya*—Don't rely on the personality of the speaker, saying, "This person is credible, so it must be so."

10. *Ma samano no garu ti*—Don't follow a teaching merely because the speaker is your respected teacher.

Instead, this teaching suggests applying critical intelligence while reflecting on the doctrines, practices, and teachers we encounter. In particular, we are asked to observe the results that arise from the practice of religious teachings, especially ethical ones. We are to develop discrimination and wisdom before developing faith; our personal experience is the laboratory in which we test the veracity of religious claims. Early in his teaching career, the Buddha proclaimed, "That which the Buddha teaches, he has realized himself through his own experience."[5] This has become the litmus test for the entire Buddhist tradition—trust in direct

---

5. Digha-nikaya I.250, *The Long Discourses of the Buddha*, translated by Maurice Walshe (Boston: Wisdom Publications, 1987, 1995), 193–94.

experience as the final measure for the efficacy of the teachings. We need to use our own experience to test not only our own tradition but also the traditions and religious claims of others.

These injunctions also relate to the Buddha's encouragement to question whatever claims might not ring true. As he says in the Discourse, "it is proper to doubt." This is not an absolute. Pervasive doubt is a real obstruction to the spiritual path, but doubt that becomes perplexity is a healthy component of inquiry, part of the motivation for further investigation. Certainty dawns only when doubt spurs a deeper inquiry.

Within the Buddhist tradition in the West, the *Kalama Sutta* has been called "The Buddha's Charter of Free Inquiry," sometimes giving rise to irreligious claims that Buddha was only a freethinker with no religious context of any kind.[6] These positions take the Buddha's advice from the *Kalama Sutta* out of the context in which these ten cautions were presented. The discourses in the Pali canon are always contextualized by the introduction that identifies the place of the teaching, the audience and setting, and the questions or circumstances that gave rise to the request for the Buddha to teach. In the context of the teaching to the Kalamas, the Buddha is speaking outside of the context of instructing his own committed students. His advice is appropriate especially for the interreligious context of a pluralistic world, addressed to anyone—whether seeker or dialogue partner—confused by competing religious claims. Don't be persuaded by charismatic gurus, philosophic reasoning, or time-honored traditions. Use your own reflection, intelligence, and the wisdom of personal experience to assess and evaluate religious teachings.

---

6. Bhikku Bodhi, "A Look at the Kalama Sutta," *Buddhist Studies: Buddha Dharma Education Association & BuddhaNet,* http://www.buddhanet.net/e-learning/kalama1_l.htm (accessed April 19, 2015).

The Discourse also suggests that promoting our own religious traditions and denigrating others creates an environment hostile to interreligious understanding and harmony. Exclusivism undermines the dignity and integrity of our own commitments even while it sows seeds of competition, prejudice, and antagonism toward religious others. Still, we are not to view all religions with agnosticism or value neutrality—it is important to see the effects that diverse religious traditions have on human life. The Buddha recommends evaluating conflicting religious claims in a specific way, based not so much on their truth or lack of truth but on the quality of the human lives of their adherents. Do the practitioners or adherents lead a wholesome life, free from greed, hatred, and delusion? Do the lifestyles of the practitioners or adherents lead to benefit and happiness for themselves and others?

At the conclusion of the Discourse, the Buddha describes the beneficial lifestyle of an adherent as "noble" when the disciple develops a heart filled with loving-kindness, compassion, joy, and equanimity, "widespread, great, boundless, free from hatred, and untroubled."[7] In the case of interreligious understanding, religious traditions have merit insofar as they yield lifestyles in which adherents are ethically motivated and develop happiness and altruism. Identifying these criteria removes us from merely intellectual, theoretical, or dogmatic perspectives about religious traditions and places emphasis on the human dimension, the way we live together in a diverse and pluralistic world.

We may ask what is missing in this presentation: how might we engage critically with the *Sutta* itself? While the Buddha weighs the veracity of teaching based on the wholesomeness of the conduct of its adherents, in this text wholesomeness is not

---

7. "Discourse to the Kalamas," 23–24.

fully defined. In Pali Buddhism wholesomeness is generally described as freedom from torturous emotions and from harming others, but are there positive descriptions of wholesome outcomes? How long does it take to be assured of the wholesomeness of a spiritual teacher's conduct, and in what situations should we observe this conduct in order to be sure of the genuineness of that person's ethical qualities?

In addition, are there no other criteria by which we can evaluate the legitimacy of the truth claims of religious others? Are there aspects other than the ethical norms of proponents by which to weigh the veracity of the tenets of their teachings? If the Buddha is removing any considerations of logic, antiquity, or common sense, is there no value placed on reasoning, philosophy, or practical thinking? This approach verges on the anti-intellectual, which raises a whole new set of issues in the interreligious arena.

Nevertheless, in my life as a dharma teacher and professor of Buddhist theology, the *Kalama-Sutta* has served as a refreshing, earthy counterpoint to the habitual tendencies of my students, who are often cut off from their ability to connect with personal experience and to evaluate the perspectives of spiritual or religious others. The appeal to experience, critical evaluation, respect for religious others, and observation of ethical conduct has provided valuable tools for them in interreligious dialogue.

QUESTIONS FOR REFLECTION/DISCUSSION

1. What role does doubt play in your spiritual life? What distinguishes healthy from unhealthy doubt?

2. How do you evaluate the religious or spiritual teachings of religious others?

3. What do you think of the ten common pitfalls that the Buddha outlines? What other considerations might you add to this list?

FOR FURTHER READING

Stephen Batchelor. *The Faith to Doubt: Glimpses of Buddhist Uncertainty.* Berkeley: Counterpoint, 2015.

Rupert Gethin. *The Foundations of Buddhism.* Oxford and New York: Oxford University Press, 1998.

Sharon Salzberg. *Insight Meditation: A Step-by-Step Course on How to Meditate.* Boulder: Sounds True, 2002.

Ajahn Sucitto. *Turning the Wheel of Truth: Commentary on the Buddha's First Teaching.* Boston: Shambhala Publications, 2010.

2

Are Religious Differences Only Semantic?

ANANTANAND RAMBACHAN

The famous Ṛg Veda text (I.164.46) "*Ekam sat viprāh bahudhā vadanti*" ("The One Being the wise speak of in many ways") is cited often by Hindus in interreligious contexts to minimize the significance of differences within and among religious traditions and to explain away these differences as entirely inconsequential and semantic.[1] Such interpretations have resulted in justifiable criticism of the Hindu approach as one that fails to properly distinguish one religious tradition from another and that relegates differences to the non-essential aspects of religion. Hindus, many protest, make light of the unique character of each of the world's religions and are not always attentive to intra-religious diversity. What can we learn from each other, one may rightly ask, if we are all, in essence, proclaiming the same truths in different words? The extensive use of this Ṛg Veda text and the problems it presents for Hindus and for persons of other religions engaged in dialogue with Hindus require that we take a closer look at the text and its context.

The meaning and significance of the text will be appreciated better if we look at the entire verse in which it occurs, as well as the preceding verse (I.164.45).

---

1. The popular translation is "The One Being the wise call by many names." "Speak of in many ways" is more faithful to the original text, *bahudhā vadanti*.

Speech hath been measured out in four divisions.
The Wise who have understanding know them.
Three kept in close concealment cause no motion;
of speech men only speak the fourth division. (45)
They call him Indra, Mitra, Varuna, Agni, and he is
    the noble-winged Garutman.
The One Being the wise speak of in many ways:
they call it Agni, Yama, Matarisvan. (46)[2]

Verse I.164.45 provides the context with an insight about the nature of human speech. It does so by presenting the totality of speech as consisting of four quarters. Human speech comprises only a quarter of the total speech potential. In describing the three quarters of speech as "kept in close concealment" and causing "no motion," the verse suggests powerfully the language of silence and the ultimate inexpressibility of the One Being referred to in the verse following (46). The text seems to suggest that articulated speech does not exhaust our modes of communication.

Contextualizing the Text
What is the religious context that we may presume for this text? Given the age of the Ṛg Veda (c.1500 BCE or earlier), the text is addressing an intra-religious situation in which the different names used for God were perceived as referring to different realities. It is also possible that claims were being made for the superiority of one name and form over another, and communities saw themselves as religious rivals. By calling attention to the oneness

---

2. *The Hymans of the Rigveda*, translated by Ralph T. H. Griffiths (Delhi: Motilal Banarsidass, reprint, 1973), translation modified.

of God and describing those who use different names as wise, the text presents us with an alternative way of interpreting the diversity of divine names and ways of speaking. The God of the other is not false, non-existent or subordinate to one's own, but a different way of naming and imagining the One Being (*ekam sat*). We choose from the many names and images of the One. It may be problematic, however, when this text is lifted from its intra-religious context, where there is a significant sharing of beliefs and practices, and applied uncritically to a new interreligious reality with more contrasting worldviews. Such a situation will necessarily require deeper dialogical engagement, and the text certainly invites such conversations across religious traditions.[3] What common ground does it require for us to say that our traditions are oriented to One Being (*ekam sat*)?

The Limits of Language

Hindu sacred texts and traditions remind us constantly that, in relation to God, our language is always limited and inadequate. God is always more than we can define, describe, or understand with our finite minds and languages. No representation of the divine in image or words can ever be complete. The implication is that we ought to profess our traditions with humility and be open always to the possibility of learning from and being enriched by the ways people of other traditions experience and describe God.

When we employ our limited language, a fraction of the total potentiality of expression, to speak of the One Being, our language will be diverse (*bahudhā*). With our finite words, we struggle to

---

3. Miroslav Volf's book *Allah: A Christian Response* (New York: HarperOne, 2011) is an excellent example of the investigation of this issue in relation to Islam and Christianity.

describe That which will always be linguistically elusive. As the Taittirīya Upaniṣad (2.4) puts it, God (*brahman*) is "That from which mind and speech return, having failed to reach." We use many names (Indra, Mitra, Varuna, Agni, Yama, Matarisvan, Garutman), not because the gods are many, but because of the limits of human language and experience. One name will never be enough. In the Hindu tradition, God as Vishṇu has at least a thousand names and so does Shiva and the divine feminine, Durgā. The different names are not just names. Each name also points to a different way of visualizing and understanding the nature of the One Being. Each is a name of the One and each emphasizes specific dimensions of the One.

The Oneness of God

Acknowledging the diversity of human names and ways of speaking about God, the Ṛg Veda text is unambiguous in its assertion that God is one (*ekam sat*). It is the one God that is spoken of differently. Those who name and worship God as Indra, Agni, or Varuna are not, in reality, addressing themselves to different beings but to the one true being. One name alone is not true and all others false, and one name does not include or represent all others. Each is a name for the One. The text rejects the literal existence of many gods and proclaims the truth of the One. At the same time, the One God is named and visualized differently within the diverse streams of Hinduism. Extended to other traditions, we may say that the text does not allow for a Jewish, Christian, Muslim, or Hindu God. It does recognize multiple understandings, while denying multiple divinities. We can speak in different—and even contradictory—ways about the One Being. The oneness of God is not compromised by the manyness of names or ways of speaking.

This insight enables us to think of persons in other traditions not as strangers with alien, false, or rival deities but as fellow beings whose God is our God. For Gandhi, this Ṛg Veda insight was transformative. "I believe," wrote Gandhi, "in the absolute oneness of God and, therefore, of humanity. What though we have many bodies? We have but one soul. The rays of the sun are many through refraction. But they have the same source. I cannot, therefore, detach myself from the wickedest soul nor may I be denied identity with the most virtuous.[4]

Differences Are Significant

Although acknowledging the limits of language and the multiple ways in which God is named, imagined, and spoken of, the Ṛg Veda text does not, as is all too commonly assumed, insist that religious differences are insignificant. There is no minimization here of religious differences or an implication that all traditions are identical. One may make the argument that the Ṛg Veda text is limited to acknowledging the many names that are used for God and does not at all address different theological understandings. This, however, is not my point of view, since each name also implies a different image and understanding.

Instead of seeing in this text an underplaying of differences, we may read from it *the necessity for attentiveness to diverse ways of speaking about God*. It is the wise (*viprāh*), after all, who speak differently about God. Theological diversity is not dismissed here as the consequence of ignorance. By acknowledging that wise people may speak differently about God, the text invites a respectful and inquiring response to religious diversity. We must not hastily and arrogantly denounce the

---

4. Mahatma Gandhi, *All Men Are Brothers* (New York: Continuum, 2001), 72.

sacred speech of the other as undeserving of sincere and serious contemplation. Wisdom must not be identified solely with our way of speaking, and we should not assume that wise persons always speak identically or that wisdom is manifested only in consensus. When encountering the ancient religious traditions of our neighbors, we would do better to assume that these traditions endure because they speak wisely and meaningfully to the human predicament and ask how we could learn from and be enriched by their distinctive ways of speaking. We will not learn, however, unless our disposition to these traditions is humble and we cease condemning that which is different. Humility is nurtured by the awareness that our ways of speaking are not exhaustive. Some of our deepest religious insights are awakened through our encounter with wise voices radically different from our own. We speak more wisely if we are open to the wisdom that flows from different sources.

All Ways of Speaking Are Not Equal

The Ṛg Veda text acknowledges that there are different ways of speaking about God, but it should not be read as affirming the equal worth of all ways of speaking. Although the text identifies the One Being as the common referent of diverse religious speech, it does not imply that each way of speaking is equally true to its referent.

Today, we are much more aware of ways of speaking in the name of God that awaken hate and instigate violence towards others within and outside our traditions. Some religious voices can legitimize injustice and oppression even as others can liberate and advocate for equality. It is naïve and dangerous to attribute equal validity to all religious voices. Even Mahatma Gandhi, a great advocate of religious diversity, found it impossible to grant equal value to all religious voices. The great Hindu failure, in Gandhi's view, was untouchability, and he could not affirm interpretations of the tradition that sanctioned its demeaning practices. Mere difference in speech is not wisdom, and we are not exempted from exercising discernment in choosing those ways of speaking about God that are conducive to the universal common good and human flourishing. By offering the insight that the One Being may be spoken of differently, the Ṛg Veda text seeks to promote peace and mutual understanding in communities of diversity.

The Simplification of the Text

Why do so many contemporary Hindu interpreters read this text in ways that minimize the significance of differences among religions and reduce these to a matter of semantics? The reasons are, in the main, historical. Although throughout the centuries the diverse traditions comprising Hinduism engaged in vigorous debates, seeking to convince the other of the truth of their claims, these traditions shared many common elements and had no organized agenda or program to entirely replace the other. Religious diversity was not intrinsically negativized, and the reality of multiple ways of being religious had been present from ancient times. India's long experience with religious diversity led to a spirit of religious accommodation and the acceptance of differences.

The entry of proselytizing religions into India with declared aims to triumph over India's ancient traditions sounded a discordant note. In contrast to traditional attitudes, these appeared aggressive, militant, and arrogant. Theological claims were articulated as being unique, exclusive, and different from India's religions. Hindus responded to these claims by representing the Hindu tradition as non-exclusive and as affirming the validity of all religions. They drew attention to what they perceived to be the common character of the world's religions in contrast to apologists who privileged their traditions and were dismissive of other traditions in their entirety. In challenging the proselytizers' claims, however, Hindu approaches to religious diversity were simplified and many of its more challenging and relevant insights overlooked. The treatment of the famous Ṛg Veda text, "The One Being the wise speak of in many ways," illustrates well this type of historical simplification and neglect of the rich resources of Hinduism for engaging in dialogue.

The Value of the Text

What then, one may rightly ask, is the value of the text, "The One Being the wise speak of in many ways"? Its value is to be found particularly in the articulation of an overlooked implication of God's oneness—the fact that my neighbor of another tradition, who speaks a different religious language, and I are addressing and relating ourselves to the same God. Through differences of name, symbols, cultures, and theologies, we comfortably clothe God with an identity that is similar to our own and fail to recognize the one God in other theological and symbolic garb.

Discerning the truth of the "One Being the wise speak of in many ways," is profoundly transformative. Thinking of my Jewish, Christian, and Muslim friends as being oriented toward the same One Being fills me with the joyous excitement of recognizing a new relationship. It enlarges my understanding of the boundaries of a religious community that now includes all who understand themselves in relation to this One Being. It motivates me to build dialogical relationships with those whose lives are centered on this One Being. I am eager to learn what my friends know of this One Being, about whom my tradition also speaks. I want to share my knowledge of the One and to be enriched by their experiences. A single text that can awaken us to the limits of our language, expand religious boundaries and horizons, foster relationships of sharing and learning, and help to overcome alienation among persons of different traditions certainly has deep historical and interreligious significance.

QUESTIONS FOR REFLECTION/DISCUSSION

1. In describing the three quarters of speech as "kept in close concealment" and causing "no motion," what do you think the Ṛg Veda hymn is suggesting?

2. What do we need to know about the nature of God in another religious tradition to decide if we worship the same God?

3. If we cannot attribute equal value to all ways of speaking about God, how do we exercise discernment?

4. What is the significance of language in interreligious relationships? How is this related to humility?

FOR FURTHER READING

Francis X. Clooney. "Hindu Views of Religious Others: Implications for Christian Theology." *Theological Studies* 64 (2003): 306–33.

Harold Coward, ed. *Modern Indian Responses to Religious Pluralism*. Albany: State University of New York Press, 1987.

Mahatma Gandhi, *All Men Are Brothers*. New York: Continuum, 2001.

Jeffrey Long. "Hinduism and the Religious Other." In *Understanding Interreligious Relations*, edited by David Cheetham, Douglas Pratt, and David Thomas, 37–63. Oxford: Oxford University Press, 2014.

Arvind Sharma. *Hinduism as a Missionary Religion*. Albany: State University of New York Press, 2011.

K. R. Sundararajan. "The Hindu Models of Interreligious Dialogue." *Journal of Ecumenical Studies* 23 (1986): 239–50.

Miroslav Volf. *Allah: A Christian Response*. New York: HarperOne, 2011.

3

Balancing Theological Exclusivism
with Metaphysical Inclusivism

Mahan Mirza

Developing a personal relationship with the Qur'an has been the formative undertaking of my adult life. I believe that it speaks to believers not simply through the meanings that are contained in its words, but also through the thoughts and feelings that are evoked in the movement from one idea to another, as well as through the rhythm contained in its recitation, or as Michael Sells terms it, in its "soundscapes." In one daily reading during the month of Ramadan, we find: "We have certainly interspersed for the people this Qur'an with every [kind of] parable" (17:89). As a practicing Muslim, I view the Qur'an as a sacred vessel through which to explore all manner of inquiry.

The verses quoted below are from the opening and closing of Sūra 64 of the Qur'an. This sūra appears toward the end of the Qur'an in a cluster of ten relatively short Medīnan sūras that summarize some of the major themes of the Qur'an. Consisting of 18 verses, the theme of S. 64 is *īmān* or faith: the first part contains the three main articles of faith in God, the Messenger (Prophet Muhammad, peace be upon him), and the Hereafter; the second part lists the fruits of true faith and things in life that can distract from it. Below, I have selected a verse from the beginning of the sūra and part of a verse from the end.

It is He who created you. One of you is an unbeliever,
and one of you a believer; and God sees the things
you do. (Q. 64:2)

So fear God as far as you are able. (Q. 64:16)

According to recent literary approaches to the Qur'an, both
traditional and scholarly, many of the sūras are designed in the
form of rings where the beginning and end mirror each other, the
center being an axis containing the core message. At the center of
Sūra 64 is an all-out call to have faith in God for the purpose of
success in the Hereafter (64:7–10), with the reminder that whatever tests and challenges befall one happen with the prior knowledge and permission of God (64:11).

Although the sūra does not take up the question of free will
and predestination directly, the "mirror" sets up a tension between
God's creative power and will in having purposefully created both
believers and disbelievers. It has been observed that the entirety
of Islamic religious thought is in a way a balancing act on a
tightrope that is sustained by just such a tension between God's
sovereignty and human responsibility. In this brief essay, I hope
to examine this tension by reflecting on the relationship of human
beings to divine truth based on their individual spiritual capacities
and natures. I hope that the thoughts presented here will help us
to see each other beyond the dichotomous categories of "believers" and "disbelievers," but as purposeful beings who are joined
together through the act of creation, each on an individually cus-
tomized path in the journey back to the Divine.

The primary source for these reflections are the Qur'anic
verses that appear above, to which I will add several more below.
I read these verses in light of our contemporary understanding of

the human as a biological organism, merging that understanding with the theological perspective that a person possesses a spiritual essence. What appears here is a brief personal reflection on the meaning of the Qur'an in light of our prevailing scientific understanding of the world. While some people might object to the mingling of these fields, it is my conviction that our readings of the Qur'an are *always* conditioned by the ways in which we understand and know the world. The Qur'an not only permits but also invites one to engage it deeply: "What, do they not ponder the Qur'an? Or is it that there are locks upon their hearts?" (47:24). It seems nonsensical to me to bracket certain domains of knowledge or experience from the interpretive enterprise. Such a move would imply a denial of *tawḥīd*, or an ultimate unity of all things. The fact that science changes is not a problem, for all human experience is contextual. Hence, it is impossible for me to think about these issues in exactly the same way that my predecessors did, and those who come after me will find entirely new reasons to be inspired by God's words in light of new knowledge. The ability of scripture to remain relevant as it moves from context to context is what makes it scripture; if great literature can do that, then *a fortiori*, scripture can do it even better.

The Qur'an teaches that "The variety of your tongues and hues is of His signs" (30:22). And, "O Mankind, We have created you male and female, and appointed you races and tribes" (49:13). All of this has been done, according to the Qur'an, to test us.

> To every one of you We have appointed a right way and an open road. If God had willed, He would have made you one nation; but that He may try you in what has come to you. So be you forward in good works; unto God shall you return, all together; and He will tell you of that whereon you were at variance. (5:48)

The text makes it abundantly clear that the world is an abode of trial: "We have appointed all that is on the earth an adornment for it, and that We may try which of them is fairest in works" (18:7). And "He is powerful over everything—who created death and life, that He might try you as to which of you is fairest in works" (67:2).

A plain-sense reading of these verses suggests that the existence of "disbelievers" in the world is at least in part purposeful because it is a source of trial for believers. How do we treat our friends, neighbors, and colleagues with whom we have fundamental disagreements about the nature of reality and the contours of the good life? How do we treat our enemies? If we all thought, believed, and behaved in the same way, we would not have to confront such questions. Without "disbelievers," the moral test of generosity toward or forgiveness of another would be severely limited, as would the virtues of fortitude, patience, and perseverance. How could it be, then, that people who play such a vital role in the grand scheme of things are to be denied God's mercy forever, as many religious adherents across traditions seem to believe?

One of the intellectual forces that challenges the frontiers of theology is our ever-changing conception of the human being. Philosophers have long wondered whether all actions are predetermined though a series of causes, propelled inexorably in a direction that has been fixed by a so-called first cause. Scientists today wonder similarly: Do our genes fix our destinies? Do they make us prone to weight gain? Is there a gene that governs sexual orientation? Am I hardwired to develop heart disease, cancer, or Alzheimer's? Is it not true that each of us responds to stimuli—mental, social, and physical—differently?

Given this knowledge, is it possible to fathom, by extension, the existence of something like a "spiritual DNA"? Could it be that some of us, depending on our spiritual DNAs, personal journeys, and communal influences, incline more to the spiritual and ethical teachings of one tradition or another? The prophet Muhammad is informed in the Qur'an: "They will question thee concerning the Spirit," to which he is guided to reply, "Say: 'The Spirit is of the bidding of my Lord. You have been given of knowledge nothing except a little'" (17:85). According to the Qur'an and Muslim tradition, human beings are the fusion of body and spirit (*rūḥ*) (15:29). Just as every person possesses physical endowments and opportunities, we each also possess spiritual capacities—and only God can judge how well each individual performs in an ultimate sense, because only He is aware of all the parameters of personal performance. In this world, we are required to judge on the basis of what is apparent but, in reality, only God knows the true station and destiny of each individual.

Regardless of one's beliefs on the question of free will and predestination, bodies "predetermine" certain things in life: a fish can breathe in water; a bird can fly; a female can bring life into the world; and a tall, athletic person can slam dunk a basketball. My question is whether there are similar limitations—or determinations—in the spiritual realm that restrict one's options to go along a particular spiritual path. If that is the case, would I be deemed a "believer" before God if I were to choose the best option *given my particular spiritual disposition* while being deemed a "disbeliever" by others who are on different paths?

The Qur'an tells the prophet Muhammad, in the verse immediately before the *rūḥ* verse just mentioned, to "Say: 'Every man works according to his own manner; but your Lord knows very well what man is best guided as to the way'" (17:84). The Arabic for manner is *shakl*—form or mold. If my genes predispose me to piety and devotion according to a particular "mold"—Christian love, Jewish covenant, Buddhist renunciation, Islamic submission—could my existence then be purposeful on account of my own personal spiritual journey while simultaneously being a challenge for others who believe differently? This is admittedly a provocative question. While not intended as an articulation of relativism in an absolute sense, it does indicate that truths may be relative in a relational sense. The mysterious interplay of body, spirit, environment, and culture exist along a spectrum whose degrees are known only to God. As Ghazali (d. 1111) and others have already taught us, a person may be a disbeliever in the eyes of people but a believer in the eyes of God, or the other way around.

By introducing this bio-eco-metaphysical perspective, we may be able to imagine new pluralist theologies that remain deeply rooted in our own respective traditions. If acceptance in God's eyes is based on an inner path and struggle known only to the One, then the labels of "believer" or "disbeliever" through an assessment of a person's outer state at any given time may apply at the worldly level, but the rules may be different at the divine level.

History has shown over and over again the destructive consequences that arise when "believers" are unable to separate their own convictions from the ultimate unknowability of Divine reality and purpose. Fervent devotees of any tradition are apt to interpret a rejection of their invitation to join their religious community as a rejection of God. What should happen, instead, is that the meaning of such a rejection needs to be reframed: (1) perhaps it is due to the weakness in the invitation made by the believer; (2) perhaps it is due to the stubbornness of the disbeliever; (3) or perhaps it is because some people are simply "created to disbelieve." The first two options have been entertained widely in the Islamic scholarly tradition. To these, I am adding the third.

A theological perspective that incorporates an understanding of and respect for differences as not necessarily negating the salvific possibilities of others may help in finding the right balance between humility and zeal. That is why my mission need not merely be an invitation to "Islam," but it may also be a call (*da'wa*) for others to live according to the best of what is contained in their own religious traditions: "Say, 'O People of the Scripture, you are on nothing until you uphold the Torah, the Gospel, and what has been revealed to you from your Lord'" (5:68). Such a call would make sense in a world that may be theologically (or doctrinally) exclusive, but metaphysically inclusive. That is to say, while religious individuals and groups passionately pursue what they consider to be God's truth, they must also understand that matters of belief can ultimately be judged only by God. Perhaps Hemingway sums it up best: "There is nothing noble in being superior to your fellow man; true nobility is being superior to your former self."

Questions for Reflection/Discussion

1. How do you understand the truth claims of your tradition in light of the multiplicity of religious and cultural traditions in the world?

2. How do you understand the relationship between theology and divine mystery?

3. Can one seek to spread the teachings of his or her religious tradition and engage in interreligious dialogue?

For Further Reading

Fred Donner. *Muhammad and the Believers: At the Origins of Islam*. Cambridge, MA: Belknap Press, 2010.

Carl Ernst. *How to Read the Qur'an: A New Guide with Select Translations*. Chapel Hill: University of North Carolina Press, 2011.

Nidhal Guessoum. *Islam's Quantum Question: Reconciling Muslim Tradition and Modern Science*. New York: IB Tauris, 2011.

Ian Markham. *A Theology of Engagement*. Hoboken, NJ: Wiley-Blackwell, 2003.

Mustansir Mir. *Coherence in the Qur'an*. Indianapolis, IN: American Trust Publications, 1987.

Ebrahim Moosa. *Ghazālī and the Poetics of Imagination*. Chapel Hill: University of North Carolina Press, 2005.

Reza Shah-Kazemi. *The Other in Light of the One: The Universality of the Qur'an and Interfaith Dialogue*. Cambridge, UK: Islamic Texts Society, 2006.

Hamza Yusuf. "Who Are the Disbelievers?" *Seasons* 5, no. 1 (Spring 2008): 31–50.

4

"The Cathedral of the World"

Interconnection in Difference

ABIGAIL CLAUHS

Rev. Dr. Forrest Church (1948–2009) was a Unitarian Universalist minister, theologian, and public intellectual. He served the Unitarian Church of All Souls in New York City from 1978 until his death in 2009. Church was a strong voice of liberal religion and social justice activism, authoring and editing more than twenty books in his lifetime, including *Our Chosen Faith: An Introduction to Unitarian Universalism*; *God and Other Famous Liberals*; and *So Help Me God: The Founding Fathers and the First Great Battle over Church and State*. As he battled with terminal cancer in the last three years of his life, Church reflected deeply on the meaning of death and dying and wrote his book, *Love and Death: My Journey through the Valley of the Shadow*. His final book, *The Cathedral of the World: A Universalist Theology*, was published posthumously. In it, he introduces his metaphor of the Cathedral of the World as a twenty-first-century Unitarian Universalist theology.

Imagine awakening one morning from a deep and dreamless sleep to find yourself in the nave of a vast cathedral . . . This cathedral is as ancient as humankind, its cornerstone the first altar, marked with the tincture of blood and blessed by tears. Search for a lifetime—which is all you are surely given—and you shall never know its limits, visit all its transepts, worship at its myriad shrines, nor span its celestial ceiling with your gaze. The builders have worked from time immemorial, destroying and creating, confounding and perfecting, tearing down and raising up arches in this cathedral, buttresses and chapels, organs, theaters and chancels, gargoyles, idols and icons...

Welcome to the Cathedral of the World.

Above all else, contemplate the windows. In the Cathedral of the World there are windows beyond number, some long forgotten, covered with many patinas of dust, others revered by millions, the most sacred of shrines. Each in its own way is beautiful. Some are abstract, others representational; some dark and meditative, others bright and dazzling. Each tells a story about the creation of the world, the meaning of history, the purpose of life, the nature of humankind, the mystery of death. The windows of the cathedral are where the light shines through.

As with all extended metaphors for meaning, this one is imperfect. The Light of God (or Truth or Being Itself, call it what you will) shines not only upon us, but out from within us as well. Together with the windows, we are part of the Cathedral, not apart from it. Together we comprise an interdependent web of being. The Cathedral is constructed out of star stuff, and so are we. We are that part (that known part) of the creation that contemplates itself, part of the poem that we ponder. Because the Cathedral is so vast, our life so short and our vision so dim, we are able to contemplate only a tiny part of the cathedral, explore a few apses, reflect upon the play of light and darkness through a few of its myriad windows. Yet, since the whole (holographically or organically) is contained in each of the parts, as we ponder and act on the insight from our ruminations, we may discover insights that will invest our days with meaning and our lives with purpose.

A twenty-first-century theology based on the concept of one Light and many windows offers to its adherents both breadth and focus. Honoring many different religious approaches, it only excludes the truth-claims of absolutists. That is because fundamentalists claim that the Light shines through their window only. Some go so far as to beseech their followers to throw stones through other people's windows.

Skeptics draw the opposite conclusion. Seeing the bewildering variety of windows and observing the folly of the worshipers, they conclude that there is no Light. But the windows are not the Light. They are where the Light shines through.

We shall never see the Light directly, only as refracted through the windows of the Cathedral. Prompting humility, life's mystery lies hidden, beyond knowledge's most ample ken. The Light (God, Truth) is veiled. Yet, that we can encompass with our minds the universe that encompasses us is a cause for great wonder. I humbly stand in the Cathedral of the World trembling with awe.[1]

I was eighteen years old, sitting in a folding chair in a small circle of people, nervous yet excited, when I first heard those words. We were in a small room adjacent to the sanctuary of Arlington Street Church, the stately brownstone Unitarian Universalist church at the corner of the Boston Public Garden, there for a class on becoming new members. The group leader had lit a

---

1. Forrest Church, *The Cathedral of the World: A Universalist Theology* (Boston: Beacon Press, 2009), xv–xvii. Copyright © 2009 by Forrest Church. Reprinted by permission of Beacon Press, Boston.

small chalice—"the symbol of our living Unitarian Universalist faith," he had told us—then opened up a book, and began reading to us those words of Forrest Church, this mysterious vision of the Cathedral of the World.

Born and raised in the Bible Belt South and recently arrived in Boston for college, I was still new to Unitarian Universalism. I had ventured into Arlington Street Church only a few weeks before, curious about what I had heard about this liberal religion. Disillusioned with the conservative Christianity of my childhood, I was seeking an open and loving spiritual community—and I immediately knew I had found it after experiencing a service at Arlington Street. Seeing the welcome that people of all abilities, races, creeds, sexualities, and genders received, and reading the Seven Principles of Unitarian Universalism,[2] I knew I was home.

What I did not know then, however, was that I was conveniently located at the heart of Unitarian Universalist history. As I sat in that room at Arlington Street Church, it was only a short walk across Boston Common and up Beacon Hill to the Unitarian Universalist Association's headquarters. A few blocks beyond that sat King's Chapel, which adopted Unitarianism in the 1780s. And directly facing Arlington Street Church, regal in his robes, stood a statue of William Ellery Channing, the great leader and preacher of Unitarianism in the early nineteenth century.

It would take some time for me to better learn this history. To realize I shared my new faith with John and Abigail Adams and

---

2. The Principles are: "1st Principle: The inherent worth and dignity of every person; 2nd Principle: Justice, equity and compassion in human relations; 3rd Principle: Acceptance of one another and encouragement to spiritual growth in our congregations; 4th Principle: A free and responsible search for truth and meaning; 5th Principle: The right of conscience and the use of the democratic process within our congregations and in society at large; 6th Principle: The goal of world community with peace, liberty, and justice for all; 7th Principle: Respect for the interdependent web of all existence of which we are a part."

other familiar names from my textbooks. To learn that Unitarianism and Universalism had been two discrete religious movements emerging from Christianity—and that they had not merged until 1961 to form the Unitarian Universalist Association of Congregations.

As my involvement with Unitarian Universalism deepened, I learned the historical theologies. How Unitarians had rejected the concept of the Trinity, seeing Jesus as fully human, a child of God only insofar as all people are children of God. How Universalists affirmed that God would save all people and condemn no one to eternal damnation. And how Unitarian minister Thomas Starr King supposedly once remarked, "Universalists believe that God is too good to damn people, and the Unitarians believe that people are too good to be damned by God."[3]

I learned about the rich history of social justice activists in our past, from abolitionists to suffragettes to martyrs who were killed by white supremacists in Selma. I discovered how, in the twentieth century, the two liberal religious movements of Unitarianism and Universalism realized their values of theological openness and social justice could form a stronger voice if merged together. I found out how, in the wake of the merger, we embraced religious pluralism and a theological exploration beyond Christianity to all the world's religions and philosophies.

The more I learned about Unitarian Universalist history and theologies, the more I appreciated Church's concept of the Cathedral of the World as a twenty-first-century reinterpretation of the historic ideas of Unitarianism and Universalism: a new Unitarianism of one light and a new Universalism of many windows.

The concept of the Cathedral of the World has also framed my approach to interreligious work. Unitarian Universalism is

3. Mark W. Harris, "Unitarian Universalist Origins: Our Historic Faith," Unitarian Universalist Association, http://www.uua.org/beliefs/history/our-historic-faith.

inherently interreligious. Our embrace of religious pluralism was one of the characteristics that first drew me to the faith. Walk into many Unitarian Universalist congregations and you will see banners of the symbols of the world's religions hanging up in the sanctuary—the dharma wheel, the Star of David, the yin and yang symbol, the crescent moon and star, the "Om" character, and many, many more. Unitarian Universalists often embrace practices and traditions from various religions, identifying with labels such as a "Buddhist-inspired Unitarian Universalist"; others feel no conflict between holding onto the religious identity they were raised with while also identifying as Unitarian Universalist (e.g., a "Jewish Unitarian Universalist" or a "Sikh Unitarian Universalist"). In fact, religious pluralism is written into the very tenets of Unitarian Universalism; we name our Six Sources of Our Living Tradition as:

1. Direct experience of that transcending mystery and wonder, affirmed in all cultures, which moves us to a renewal of the spirit and an openness to the forces which create and uphold life;

2. Words and deeds of prophetic women and men which challenge us to confront powers and structures of evil with justice, compassion, and the transforming power of love;

3. Wisdom from the world's religions which inspires us in our ethical and spiritual life;

4. Jewish and Christian teachings which call us to respond to God's love by loving our neighbors as ourselves;

5. Humanist teachings which counsel us to heed the guidance of reason and the results of science, and warn us against idolatries of the mind and spirit;

6. Spiritual teachings of Earth-centered traditions which celebrate the sacred circle of life and instruct us to live in harmony with the rhythms of nature.[4]

From a tradition historically rooted in Christianity, our sources and inspiration have expanded to include wisdom from traditions around the globe.

Our Unitarian Universalist hymnal, *Singing the Living Tradition,* is used by Unitarian Universalist congregations around the world, and it includes songs and readings from many traditions, including Christianity, Judaism, Buddhism, Islam, Sikhism, and Taoism. One of our major religious education programs for Unitarian Universalist youth is a world religions program called "Building Bridges," where youth learn about other world religions. The stated goals of Building Bridges speak powerfully to how Unitarian Universalists value religious pluralism. The program's goals include the following: to "[i]ncrease knowledge of religions practiced around the world and in local communities," "[f]oster acceptance of the diverse forms that religious expression takes," "[b]uild awareness of the diversity of followers within every faith; understand that to know someone's religious identity is not the same as knowing what that person thinks, believes, or practices," and "[e]mpower youth to better appreciate human diversity and connect with others and be able to respectfully discuss important matters with people with whom they disagree."[5] We as Unitarian Universalists aim to learn about, accept, and connect across religious difference—from the lived experience of lay

---

4. "Sources of Our Living Tradition," Unitarian Universalist Association, http://www.uua.org/beliefs/what-we-believe/sources.

5. "Building Bridges: A World Religions Program," Unitarian Universalist Association, http://www.uua.org/re/tapestry/youth/bridges.

Unitarian Universalists to the official sources, publications, and curricula from the Unitarian Universalist Association.

For us, however, our Unitarian Universalist approach to religious pluralism is not without its pitfalls. There are dangers of cultural appropriation and risks of erasing differences between traditions, mixing and matching and claiming that all religions are really the same, deep down. This is where I find the Cathedral of the World to be a useful metaphor for engaging different religions.

At first glance, the Cathedral of the World might seem just as problematic—something akin to the "one mountain, many paths" approach that claims that all religions are just different paths up the same mountain and leading to the same summit. The metaphor of the mountain asserts that, at their core, all religions are really the same and lead to the same end (usually a variant of Christianity). The Cathedral of the World, however, does not try to say that all religions are the same. Instead, it acknowledges the difference and diversity of each window and the unique way each provides an understanding of the world. As people look through their windows, shaped by stories and history and culture and spirituality, they see the world in myriad different ways.

At the same time, the Cathedral of the World affirms our interconnectedness. In Church's Cathedral, all of human religious history is part of a complex whole, building upon older concepts, sharing influences, and embodying the diversity of many different contexts. It reflects the historical perspective that recognizes the interconnected development of religions. The human family shares this cathedral—and has done so for all of human history, cooperating in the work of building religious traditions together. Church recognizes that religions are not static monoliths, but rather ongoing processes. The Cathedral is ever being built and ever-changing, as new generations enter its halls.

The Cathedral of the World is a framework that calls us to recognize both our interconnectedness and our difference. Together, we—all of humanity—inhabit and create the Cathedral, yet the windows we build and through which we look at the world are very different.

And, perhaps most important to a graduate student like me, constantly steeped in academic theory—the Cathedral of the World leaves room for transcendent mystery, or what Rudolf Otto once called the *numinous,* in the form of the light. The metaphor leaves space for interpretation as to what the light—which shines from within ourselves as well as from without the Cathedral—is. Church is not claiming to have all the answers about soteriology or eschatology or any of the other "-ology" quandaries that occupy so many theologians. Rather, he is providing the image of light as a connective and mystical force that illuminates all of us in different ways, without making a truth claim about it.

To me, this light is at the core of all interreligious work. It is the ultimate mystery, a mystery about which we gain insights together through interreligious exchange. The discoveries and revelations that happen in interreligious encounters are all part of our shared journey toward understanding this light. No religion has a monopoly on the light or approaches closer to it. Rather, the light in the Cathedral of the World—which originates both from beyond human existence and from within ourselves, connecting everything together—animates and inspires the rich spectrum of human religious thought and experience of which we are all a part.

Now, you may be thinking, "This is a pretty metaphor...but why is it so important?" As a grassroots interfaith organizer and Unitarian Universalist minister-in-training, I have been involved in plenty of "on-the-ground" actions, from interreligious service projects to protests to vigils. I have found, in these settings, that it is useful to have a metaphor or an image to use in order to explain your perspective on religious diversity to people in the moment, rather than getting bogged down in dense academic explanations. Holding a picket sign or handing out sandwiches, unsurprisingly, is not the best time to unload a list of theologians and book titles on a person seeking genuine connection and understanding. Painting a verbal picture, however, has been more effective. Visual metaphors have value in explaining the ineffable or exceptionally complicated.

Church's book sits on the shelf next to my desk, and I have lent it out many times to friends and colleagues involved in interreligious work, most of them from traditions other than Unitarian Universalism. Many have found it helpful. I go back and re-read it often, when I need to remember the sacredness of the work we do.

I believe deeply in the power of interreligious engagement to transform the world, from oppressive systems to our hearts. I envision a future when we all work across religious lines for justice and wholeness and life abundant. And to do that, I believe, we must have a way to communicate how we understand our relationships to each other's religious traditions. For me, it is the Cathedral of the World. As I conceive of it—together we talk, together we work toward justice, and together we live, illuminated by the light as it shines through our manifold windows, diverse and interconnected.

QUESTIONS FOR REFLECTION/DISCUSSION

1. The Cathedral of the World is simply one metaphor for understanding the relationships between the world's religions. What metaphors do you find helpful in thinking about interreligious work?

2. Forrest Church called the concept of the Cathedral of the World a "twenty-first-century theology," reinterpreting the traditional concepts of Unitarianism and Universalism for a new millennium. How are some of the theologies or approaches of your religious tradition being transformed in the face of a twenty-first-century world that is increasingly globalized, interconnected, and interreligious?

3. What is the role of mystery in your spiritual life? Are there texts on the subject that are particularly important to you?

For Further Reading

John Buehrens and Rebecca Ann Parker. *House for Hope: The Promise of Progressive Religion for the Twenty-first Century.* Boston: Beacon Press, 2011.

Forrest Church. *The Cathedral of the World: A Universalist Theology.* Boston: Beacon Press, 2009.

Peter Morales, ed. *The Unitarian Universalist Pocket Guide.* Boston: Skinner House, 2012.

Susan J. Richie. *Children of the Same God: The Historical Relationship Between Unitarianism, Judaism, and Islam.* Boston: Skinner House, 2014.

5

Acts 2 and Interreligious Engagement

Pentecostal and Evangelical Reflections

AMOS YONG AND TIMOTHY T. N. LIM

This essay draws insights from Acts 2 for Christian interreligious engagement. Amos writes as a Pentecostal theologian who has been involved in Buddhist-Christian scholarship in the North American academy.[1] Timothy is an Evangelical-Brethren and a Presbyterian ecumenist who has had personal experience dialoguing with Asian Buddhists and Chinese religious practitioners, having been a former convert from Buddhism and working partly as a comparative theologian.[2] We hope to show from our reading of Acts 2 that Christians can engage constructively across lines of differences as faithful followers of Christ in a multireligious world. We begin with Acts 2 and a brief introduction to the text. Thereafter, we make a case for interreligious friendship, learning, and action.

---

1. See Amos Yong, *Pneumatology and the Christian-Buddhist Dialogue: Does the Spirit Blow through the Middle Way?* Studies in Systematic Theology 11 (Leiden and Boston: Brill, 2012), and *The Cosmic Breath: Spirit and Nature in the Christianity-Buddhism-Science Trialogue,* Philosophical Studies in Science & Religion 4 (Leiden and Boston: Brill, 2012).

2. See Timothy T. N. Lim, "On Overcoming Minetic and Contagion Violence," in *Faith in an Age of Terror*, ed. Quek Tze Ming and Philip E. Satterthwaite (Singapore: Genesis Books and Biblical Graduate School of Theology, 2018), 73–89.

Acts 2:1–41[3]

1 When the day of Pentecost had come, they were all together in one place. 2 And suddenly from heaven there came a sound like the rush of a violent wind, and it filled the entire house where they were sitting. 3 Divided tongues, as of fire, appeared among them, and a tongue rested on each of them. 4 All of them were filled with the Holy Spirit and began to speak in other languages, as the Spirit gave them ability. 5 Now there were devout Jews from every nation under heaven living in Jerusalem. 6 And at this sound the crowd gathered and was bewildered, because each one heard them speaking in the native language of each... about God's deeds of power." 12 All were amazed and perplexed, saying to one another, "What does this mean?"... 14 But Peter, standing with the eleven,... addressed them,... 16 "... this is what was spoken through the prophet Joel:

17 'In the last days it will be, God declares,
that I will pour out my Spirit upon all flesh,
 and your sons and your daughters shall prophesy,
and your young men shall see visions,
 and your old men shall dream dreams.
18 Even upon my slaves, both men and women,
 in those days I will pour out my Spirit;
  and they shall prophesy.
19 And I will show portents in the heaven above
 and signs on the earth below,
  blood, and fire, and smoky mist.
20 The sun shall be turned to darkness
 and the moon to blood,

---

3. New Revised Standard Version.

before the coming of the Lord's great and
glorious day.
21 Then everyone who calls on the name of the Lord
shall be saved.'

22 "You that are Israelites, listen ... : Jesus of Nazareth, a
man attested to you by God with deeds of power, wonders,
and signs that God did through him among you ...
23 this man, handed over to you according to the definite plan and foreknowledge of God, you crucified and
killed by the hands of those outside the law. 24 But God
raised him up, having freed him from death, because it
was impossible for him to be held in its power ... 32 This
Jesus God raised up, and of that all of us are witnesses.
33 Being therefore exalted at the right hand of God, and
having received from the Father the promise of the Holy
Spirit, he has poured out this that you both see and
hear ... 38 ... Repent, and be baptized every one of you
in the name of Jesus Christ so that your sins may be for-
given; and you will receive the gift of the Holy Spirit.
39 For the promise is for you, for your children, and for
all who are far away, everyone whom the Lord our God
calls to him." ... 41 So those who welcomed his message were baptized ...

A Brief Introduction

In the Christian New Testament, the Acts of the Apostles is received
as a sequel to the Gospel according to Luke, the latter having been
written to introduce the person and teachings of Jesus Christ to a
certain Theophilus. The author of both documents, a physician and
informal historian named Luke, seeks to provide a comprehensive
account of Jesus and his followers (Luke 1:1–4; Acts 1:1; 28:22).
No consensus exists as to whether Theophilus is a Christian, but
most scholars agree that he was a respectable Roman court official.

However, there is no scholarly unanimity regarding whether Acts pre-dates or post-dates the Jewish revolt and the destruction of the temple and city of Jerusalem in 70 CE. Acts has been handed down as a reliable historical record of the early church.

Acts 2 is paramount for Christians of all persuasions, albeit understood differently across the traditions. Some read Acts 2 as the start of the early church (because the Spirit was given to the believers after Jesus' ascension), while others believe the record affirms the assembling of God's people from Christianity's cradle in Judaism.[4] After Jesus' crucifixion and death, his Jewish followers lost all hope that Jesus was the prophesied messiah who would liberate the Jews from their political oppressors. So, after Jesus' ascension (Acts 1:6–11), 120 of them gathered to pray and ponder what it meant that he had instructed them to wait for the Holy Spirit to come upon them so they could be his witnesses "both in Jerusalem, and in all Judea and Samaria, and even to all ends of the earth" (Acts 1:8). Then at the Jewish feast of Pentecost (or *Shavuot*), also the Feast of the Weeks associated with the wheat harvest in the Old Testament (Exodus 23:16; Deuteronomy 16:9–12), these followers received the promised Holy Spirit in a dramatic way. The outpouring of the Spirit on the day of Pentecost not only attested to Jesus Christ's earthly ministry, but also emboldened his followers to share their faith. In time, mainstream Jews expelled these believers in Jesus as messiah from their community and the synagogue.

The Acts 2 narrative suggests that those filled with the Spirit included not only the 120 Jewish disciples of Jesus but also a group of Hellenistic Jews who had gathered in Jerusalem to celebrate the feast (vv. 9–11). Beyond the "devout Jews from every nation under heaven" (v. 5) present, there were also proselytes

---

4. John Drane, *Introducing the New Testament*, 3rd ed. (Fortress, 2010).

(v. 10), converts to the Jewish faith. Perhaps some, if not many of these, would have, in their former lives, worshiped the ancient Greek gods or participated in the mystery cults of the Roman Empire. According to Peter's explanatory speech in Acts 2, the outpouring of the Spirit fulfills the Abrahamic promise not only for the Jewish audience and their descendants but also for those who are "far away" (v. 39).[5] Whatever they may have repudiated about their former religious commitments, they were surely also shaped and informed as followers of Jesus by those experiences.

The earliest Christian devotion to and worship of Jesus Christ as the Lord (*kyrios*), attested in records of hymns (e.g., Philippians 2:6–11; Colossians 1:15–20; John 1:1–18; Ephesians 5:4; 1 Timothy 3:16), reflects the practice of adapting the title from the veneration of the Roman emperor for Christian purposes.[6] In effect, the Gospel of Jesus Christ emerged from out of a religiously pluralistic first century CE context. Arguably, the Spirit was given to enable Jesus' followers to proclaim the truth about him and the message of salvation in the multireligious Hellenistic world (and beyond).

Interpreting Acts 2 for Interreligious Friendship, Learning, and Action

Acts 2 introduces the origins, message, and mission of the church. It also exhibits an early formulation of the Christian liturgy of

---

5. Heidi J. Hirnik and Mikeal C. Parsons, "Philological and Performative Perspectives on Pentecost," in *Reading Acts Today*, ed. Steve Walton, Thomas E. Phillips, Lloyd Keith Pietersen, and F. Scott Spencer (New York: Bloomsbury T & T Clark, 2011, pbk., 2013), 137–53, esp. 139.

6. Oscar Cullman, *Early Christian Worship* (London: SCM, 1959, rpr., 1969); Jack T. Sanders, *The New Testament Christological Hymns* (Cambridge, UK: Cambridge University Press, 1971); Larry Hurtado, *Lord Jesus Christ* (Grand Rapids, MI: Eerdmans, 2005); Andrew Walls, "The Ephesian Moment," in *The Cross-Cultural Process in Christian History* (Maryknoll, NY: Orbis Books, 2002), 72–83.

repentance and baptism for the remission of sins (v. 38). In this essay, we would like to show how Acts 2 also provides insights for conceiving interreligious friendship, learning, and action.

From the perspective of the modern Pentecostal and charismatic renewal movement, Acts 2 is read as central to the ongoing outpouring of the Spirit that redeems the many tongues and languages of the world for the sake of the Gospel.[7] While Christian understandings of the nature of salvation (soteriology) and the church (ecclesiology) are the primary correlates of the pneumatological themes (those dealing with the Holy Spirit) in this text,[8] it is also possible to extrapolate implications with regard to other concerns, such as theology of creation, public theology, and, most importantly for our purposes, theology of religions.[9] If the Spirit has been poured out on all flesh (Acts 2:17) and this was made manifest with the early believers speaking in the languages of the known world, then the theological implication is that this involves the inclusion and embrace of the distinctive languages of all peoples. Further, since human languages cannot

7. Amos Yong, *Who Is the Holy Spirit?* (Brewster, MA: Paraclete Press, 2011), 12–15; Yong, *The Spirit Poured Out on All Flesh* (Grand Rapids, MI: Baker Academic, 2005), ch. 4.

8. As emphasized by Timothy T. N. Lim, "The Holy Spirit in *Evangelii Gaudium, Together Towards Life* and The Cape Town Commitment," *International Review of Mission* 104:2 (2015): 203–16; and Lim, "Towards a Protestant Pneumatological–Ecclesiology: Outside the 'Two Lungs of the Church,'" *Review of Ecumenical Studies* 7:2 (2015): 211–29.

9. See, for example, Amos Yong, *The Spirit of Creation: Modern Science and Divine Action in the Pentecostal-Charismatic Imagination* (Grand Rapids and Cambridge, UK: William B. Eerdmans Publishing Company, 2011); Yong, *In the Days of Caesar: Pentecostalism and Political Theology* (Grand Rapids and Cambridge, UK: William B. Eerdmans Publishing Company, 2010). And, regarding theology of religions, see Yong, *Discerning the Spirit(s): A Pentecostal-Charismatic Contribution to Christian Theology of Religions*, Journal of Pentecostal Theology Supplement Series 20 (Sheffield, UK: Sheffield Academic Press, 2000); *Beyond the Impasse: Toward a Pneumatological Theology of Religions* (Grand Rapids: Baker Academic, 2003); and *Hospitality and the Other: Pentecost, Christian Practices, and the Neighbor*, Faith Meets Faith series (Maryknoll, NY: Orbis Books, 2008).

be separated completely from their cultural and religious dimensions, such acceptance potentially, if not actually, extends to human cultural and religious realities as well. Hence the religions might be understood as "instruments of the Holy Spirit working out the divine purposes in the world,"[10] with implications for Christian faith and practice, especially in terms of relating to people of other faiths. An understanding of the Spirit's presence in creation and potential influence in other religions cautions against "Christians pronouncing judgment on the religions without knowing what it is they are actually making pronouncement about."[11] Instead, perhaps a contrary approach is invited: "the church will...be a servant to the religions, seeking after and contributing toward their welfare...By challenging other faiths to be true to their original commitments, enabling their reform or purification from corrupting elements, or empowering their contribution to human well-being and flourishing."[12]

We thus recommend approaching interreligious conversations with a spirit of extending hospitality in welcome, word, and deed.[13] The Pentecost message of Acts 2 invites Christians both to boldly proclaim the truth about Jesus as the Christ and to be open to following after the Spirit who will lead them into all truth, even the truth of religious others. This proposal of hospitality offered to and received from religious others is surely not the only Pentecostal or Evangelical model of interreligious engagement, especially since modern Pentecostals and Evangelicals have more often appeared to be less dialogical and much more confrontational in engaging people of other faiths. Yet our reading of Acts 2 inclines us toward friendship, learning, and collaboration with religious others.

---

10. Yong, *The Spirit Poured Out on All Flesh*, 236.

11. Ibid.

12. Ibid., 266.

13. This is the argument in Yong, *Hospitality and the Other*, chs. 3–5.

In the present time of global interreligious hostilities and conflict, our recommendation emphasizes identification of the truths and values Christians share with all other religious people as members of the human race. An important task thus involves developing the posture of learning from the religious other. Our reading of Acts 2 foregrounds a pneumatological logic—in effect a strategy for Christian reading and thinking based on the pentecostal outpouring of the Spirit on all peoples—for approaching and engaging religious others beyond the practical urgencies demanded by our twenty-first-century context.

A pneumatological model is relevant precisely because it enables us to hold in tension two responsibilities: the call to evangelism and the call to dialogical witness.[14] Followers of Christ who have received of his Spirit at Pentecost cannot but understand themselves as God's instrument to proclaim the salvific message of Christ to the non-religious and to members of other faiths, and the proclamation involves both evangelistic and non-evangelistic forms of witness. A pneumatological approach recognizes that the Spirit blows where the Spirit desires, and that human creatures can only be faithful in bearing witness to the belief in a God who saves. Yet any overt forms of evangelism have to be undertaken with an awareness of and sensitivity to the many contexts of encounter, especially those that are more politically volatile, with humility of spirit, and with respect for the (religious) freedom and dignity of others.[15]

---

14. See part 4 of Amos Yong, *The Missiological Spirit: Christian Mission Theology for the Third Millennium Global Context* (Eugene, OR: Cascade Books, 2014).

15. There are guidelines established for interreligious dialogue, but none so far on "proselytism"—what we here call *evangelism*—in a religiously plural world; for initial considerations, see Martin E. Marty and Frederick E. Greenspahn, eds., *Pushing the Faith: Proselytism and Civility in a Pluralistic World* (New York: Crossroad, 1988); see also, more recently, Indunil Janakaratne Kodithuwakku Kankanamalage, "Conversion and Proselytism in the Light of 'Christian Witness in a Multi-religious World,'" *International Review of Mission* 103, no. 1 (2014): 109–15.

On the other side is the import, in our time, of dialogical witness.[16] Such an approach listens to others so that their own tongue and witness is clearly registered, and even learns from others, although that does not mean necessarily that theological agreement with others follows. Insofar as Christians are called to be instruments of peace and heralds of the gospel in as winsome a manner as possible, current interreligious engagement would benefit from seeking harmonious relations and building solidarity toward human well-being and flourishing.

Our objective here is not to say that all religions have an identical understanding of what Christians understand by salvation. Rather, a pneumatological approach to religions might allow appreciation of other faiths in ways that neither annul Christian understandings nor contradict the Christian commitment to the finality of Christ. We view such a pneumatological method as complementary to present developments in the field of comparative theology wherein interreligious reflection does not necessarily seek to find convergence, agreement, and assimilation between religions, but fosters appreciation of similarities amidst or across differences.[17] Even if some might believe that the Spirit's work across religions leads to convergence between faiths, we would do well to grant that divergence remains a real and possible trajectory coming out of the comparative theological task and the interreligious dialogue.

It has to be said that the struggle for recognition between groups is not only multidimensional but also includes interreligious dynamics.[18] The search for and the naming of the Spirit's activity in other religions could potentially be read by the reli-

16. As in Amos Yong, *The Dialogical Spirit: Christian Reason and Theological Method for the Third Millennium* (Eugene, OR: Cascade Books, 2014), esp. parts 3 and 4.

17. Cf. Francis X. Clooney, ed., *The New Comparative Theology: Interreligious Insights from the Next Generation* (New York: Bloomsbury Publishers, 2010).

18. See Timothy Lim, *Ecclesial Recognition with Hegelian Philosophy, Social Psychology, and Continental Political Theory* (Leiden and Boston: Brill, 2017).

gious other as a form of domination over or imposition of one's superordinate perspective of the Spirit on another. Our goal, however, is not only to provide fellow Christians with theological warrants for interfaith engagement but also to open up dialogue that can both inform and transform Christian self-understanding vis-à-vis other faiths. The point of a pneumatological theology of interreligious encounter is to insist on the importance of receiving the witness of others of faith in their own tongues, and hence not to impose our perspectives on them nor dominate them. The desired outcomes always include interreligious understanding, if not also friendship, learning, and collaboration.

With this in mind, let us celebrate "the promise of the Holy Spirit" that has been poured out for us all since the first Pentecost, and perhaps we can also welcome the continuing infilling and indwelling work of the Spirit in the life of believers to, "Go, make disciples of all nations, baptizing them in the name of the Father, of the Son, and of the Holy Spirit" in an interreligiously sensitive and respectful manner, all the while extending hospitality and love as Christ's witnesses to people of all nationalities, races, ethnicities, and religions.

QUESTIONS FOR REFLECTION/DISCUSSION

1. How might a pneumatological reading of Acts 2 facilitate possibilities for interreligious friendship, learning, and collaboration? What challenges does it present?

2. What other biblical and theological resources would support a hospitable Christian interreligious engagement that, while affirming the finality of Christ, also invite interreligious dialogue and cooperation?

3. How would you describe your own theological approach to other religious traditions?

FOR FURTHER READING

Catherine Cornille. *The Im-Possibility of Interreligious Dialogue.* New York: Crossroad, 2008.

D. A. Carson. *The Gagging of God.* Grand Rapids, MI: Zondervan, 2002.

Veli-Matti Kärkkäinen. *Trinity and Religious Pluralism.* Farnham, UK: Ashgate, 2004.

Gerald R. McDermott and Harold A. Netland. *A Trinitarian Theology of Religions.* Oxford, UK: Oxford University Press, 2014.

Tony Richie. *Speaking by the Spirit: A Pentecostal Model for Interreligious Dialogue.* Lexington, KY: Emeth, 2011.

6

Wrestling with Chosenness

A Personal Reflection

NANCY FUCHS KREIMER

Mordecai Menahem Kaplan (1881–1983) was one of the great Jewish thinkers of the twentieth century. An immigrant to the United States from Russia (via France), Kaplan dedicated his life to reconstructing the basic concepts of Judaism—God, Torah, and Israel—so that they could continue to be meaningful to modern Jews in a Western democracy like America. His purpose was not to diminish the tradition, but rather to inspire in Jews a renewed identification with the Jewish people and with a Jewish way of life. He understood Judaism, like all other religions, as a historical construct that evolved over time in response to human needs.

Kaplan's magnum opus, *Judaism as a Civilization* (1934), in some ways a period piece from another era, continues to be read as a classic of modern Jewish thought. Although Kaplan's followers created what looks like another (small) denomination of American Jewry, over the years, Reconstructionists have aspired to be more a movement than a sect. In fact, Kaplan's writings continue to be a source of generative ideas and programs that enrich and enliven Jewish life across the denominational spectrum and beyond.

Unless we believe that God has revealed only to the Jews the way of life that expresses the divine goal of human evolution, we cannot honestly affirm belief in the Chosen People idea. There is no interpreting away the invidious distinction between Jews and Gentiles that such a distinction implies.

... Any religious group has the right to believe that it alone possesses the key to salvation. If we believe in freedom of religion, we must accord them that right. But, is it ethically right, in view of the invidious assumption of superiority inherent in the Chosen People idea? We deem it unethical to advance that claim on behalf of the Jewish People, and, by the same token, we find it ethically objectionable when others advance that claim.

[Thus,] the traditional formula concerning Israel's divine election is objectionable, on rational and on pragmatic grounds. Rationally, it has no place in a universe of discourse in which the belief in the supernatural revelation has become obsolete. Practically, it is objectionable as barring the way to peace and harmony among religions and making for self-righteousness and cant.[1]

Kaplan's statement on chosenness is now almost a century old. This particular aspect of his thought has proved to be, of all his contributions, one of the most provocative. On the one hand, few if any of the other Jewish movements have followed the Reconstructionists in making radical changes to liturgy to expunge references to God "choosing the Jews from among all other peoples," or blessing God for "separating between Israel and the nations." On the other hand, Kaplan's desire to reimagine chosenness permeates the thinking of many Jews today, in particular those involved in the work of interfaith engagement.

---

1. Mordecai Kaplan, *Questions Jews Ask: Reconstructionist Answers* (New York: Reconstructionist Press, 1966), 205–9.

When Kaplan first wrote about chosenness, Jews were, for the most part, still a "community of fate." American Jews, not to mention Jews in the rest of the world, were still struggling for acceptance in the wider society. Intermarriage was rare, and synagogues, Jewish centers, and Jewish neighborhoods were filled with people whose parents were both Jewish. In the current era of "post-ethnic America," our understanding of Jewish peoplehood is evolving. What do we make of Kaplan's ideas today in the context of our multifaith and multicultural society?

Kaplan's statement on chosenness, one that seeks to overturn a longstanding core Jewish tradition, was, in fact, *my* tradition as a child. In other words, I grew up knowing the ideas in this (radical) text as the Truth (capital "T"), and other, more conventional ideas on the subject as outdated notions believed by "other" Jews. Growing up in a "classical" Reconstructionist community in the 1960s (when there were still less than a dozen congregations affiliated with the movement), I was well aware that on this issue we departed from the beliefs of most other Jews, past and present.

As a young girl preparing for my bat mitzvah, I could not judge the theological virtue of one formulation over the other. But it was clear that something was up, something worth making a fuss over. When I attended the b'nai mitzvah of my friends at other synagogues, they said a different blessing before the Torah reading. This particular change was one that we alone among Jewish movements made in our prayers. Our kind of Judaism was different, and the issue of chosenness was at the core of this difference. I felt a special kinship with other Reconstructionists who shared this unique, slightly better, version of Judaism. One might even say we were, in our own eyes, "chosen" Jews. I didn't understand that bit of irony then, but it now brings a smile to my face.

In time, I did come to understand much of what Mordecai Kaplan wanted to convey to modern Jews. First, we Jews had a story to tell about ourselves that included an idea of being the chosen people of God. But this story was not Truth with a capital "T," only *our* truth. Therefore, we were free to leave out or radically upend this idea or others that did not make sense in our time and place, and to lift up other aspects of the story that worked better. Second, and related, our story was just one of many stories out there about religious communities and their relationship with God. If we understood ourselves to have an intimate relationship with God, other peoples too could feel this. They were not the "unchosen"; they simply had their own stories to tell.

I got it. In fact, so fully did I get it that I went on to study comparative religion in college, to receive a master's degree from a Christian seminary, and to write a PhD dissertation in a religion department whose specialty was interreligious studies. I also became a Reconstructionist rabbi and, with my husband, raised two daughters in a Reconstructionist congregation. I really got it! But *it* gets a bit more complicated.

Ironically, my work in the interfaith world has forced me to return, repeatedly, to the issue of chosenness. When I began to study, dialogue, and organize with Christians, I learned to my surprise that while I did not believe in the chosenness of the Jewish people, many of them did. Over the years, I noticed in conversations about the State of Israel, in particular, that this idea took two forms. Christians did not invent these two versions of the idea of election; they are present in Judaism as well. One version sees the Jewish people as especially blessed by God, having a divinely assured relationship to the Land of Israel (Genesis 15:18–21). In the other version, chosenness means heightened responsibility; the Jewish people have to conform to rigorous spiritual and ethical standards or they will (indeed, should) lose their right to the land (Deuteronomy 11:12; Leviticus 18:28). Thus, as "the elect of God," we Jews could not just be ordinary people in an ordinary country. In discussions with Christians, I often felt that some asked too little of us, while others asked too much.

Whether I liked it or not, some Christians were not about to simply drop this tenet of their faith. Even among Christians who did not believe in a God who literally chooses a people, the residue of that belief could persist, in some cases as philo-Semitism and in others as a subtle form of anti-Semitism (and sometimes as both). Neither was very helpful, in my view, but I could not wish it away by simply reading to them the writings of Mordecai Kaplan.

I realized, too, that, just as in the case with Christians, questions of chosenness continued to exist in nuanced and complicated forms among religious and secular members of the Jewish community (including my fellow Reconstructionists). I began to feel uncomfortable with my splitting of Jews into the "good ones" who shared my enlightened opinions and the "bad ones" who did not. I had a tendency to project problematic attitudes onto the others and fail to notice them among my own sub-groups. Further, I unwittingly limited the range of Jews with whom I was involved in meaningful theological and ethical discussions.

I now try to resist the temptation to claim only the parts of Judaism that I believe in, or only the people who share my beliefs and practices. Sometimes it is difficult to engage with Jewish ideas that make me uncomfortable or with Jewish people whose views differ from mine. But I remind myself that this is a virtue I have tried to cultivate regarding other faiths. I may disagree with, even deplore, certain ideas and behaviors of my fellow Jews, but I try—in the interest of pluralism—to grapple with a broader range of my tradition and of my community.

I also seek out interfaith opportunities where people confront with honesty our own rich, complex, multivalent religious heritages. I have valued those times when Jews and Christians (and, more recently, Muslims as well) share with one another our sacred texts and traditions, both the beautiful and the troubling. Or, to put it another way, texts and traditions that can be (and have been) read in troubling ways. In such contexts, we speak frankly about the light and shadow of our respective traditions. In these discussions, I join with my colleagues of other faiths as we each look for ways to tell our stories without disparaging each other's communities and beliefs. To paraphrase the late Lutheran bishop Krister Stendahl, we are learning to sing our song to God without telling negative stories about others.[2]

Such interreligious experiences have led to me to ask anew if some versions of chosenness can co-exist with a deep pluralism. Rabbi Lord Jonathan Sacks, chief rabbi of the United Hebrew Congregations of the Commonwealth, tried to accomplish just that. In the first edition of his 2002 book, *The Dignity of Difference*, he wrote:

> The truth at the beating heart of monotheism is that God is greater than religion; that He is only partially comprehended by any faith. He is my God, but also your God. He is on my side, but also on your side. He exists not only in my faith, but also in yours.[3]

In 2003, he published a second edition in which that passage, along with a score of others, had been modified. His Orthodox Jewish community told him he had pushed the envelope too far

---

2. See Krister Stendahl, "Why I Love the Bible," *Harvard Divinity Bulletin* 35, no. 1 (Winter 2007) annotated on *Genius.com*: https://genius.com/Krister-stendahl-why-i-love-the-bible-annotated.

3. Jonathan Sacks, *The Dignity of Difference: How to Avoid the Clash of Civilizations* (London: Bloomsbury Academic, 2002), 56.

and had lost sight of chosenness.[4] In his introduction to the second edition he explained that he had been misunderstood. Chosenness was secure.

More recently, Rabbi Arthur Green addressed this question from a different angle in his book *Radical Judaism*. Among the most "radical" aspects of this book is his expansive notion of the term "Israel."[5] While Green affirms the need for religious and ethnic particularism and a deepening of contemporary Jewish life and practice, he also seeks to create a greater sense of kinship and connection among diverse seekers by suggesting that the biblical meaning of Israel, "one who wrestles with God" (Genesis 32:27), can be used to describe a variety of people whose struggle for meaning and goodness lead them into contact with Jews and Judaism:

> Who is my Israel? . . . You indeed, are my Israel. You for whom I write, you whom I teach, you with whom I share a deep kinship of shared human values and love for this Jewish language. Are you all Jews in the formal sense? I'm not much worried about that question.[6]

Of course, such theological moves do worry some Jews. They argue that now more than ever we need a clear statement of the special status of the Jewish people—Israel. They fear that if we broaden such definitions too much, Jews will lose their rationale for staying together as a people.

---

4. See Sacks, *The Dignity of Difference*, revised edition (London: Bloomsbury Academic, 2003), 59.

5. See Shaul Magid's reflections on this issue in his review essay, "(Re) Reading Radicalism: Reading Reviews of Arthur Green's *Radical Judaism*," *Zeek* (March 10, 2011), http://zeek.forward.com/articles/117106/.

6. Arthur Green, *Radical Judaism: Rethinking God and Tradition* (New Haven, CT: Yale University Press, 2010), 132.

Interestingly, Mordecai Kaplan believed just the opposite. He thought the idea of divine election had the paradoxical effect of making Jews overly confident about our survival, making it *less* likely that we would have the incentive to make our Judaism meaningful. He feared the danger of falling back on our special status as justification for our continued existence. Giving up that claim, he argued, would be advantageous precisely because it would challenge us to create better answers to the question "Why belong?"

In the meantime, the Jewish people continue to evolve. The Jewish communities I inhabit are now made up of a "mixed multitude": those born of two Jewish parents or one or none, those who, for various reasons and varying lengths of time, are journeying with us Jews, with or without formal conversion. Today, when we speak of non-Jews, we are speaking not only of strangers, acquaintances, friends, or even relatives of people in our pews, but often of the people *in* the pews themselves.

With this variety in our midst, messages about Jewish specialness take on a new significance. It feels even more important to me to clarify that we view our connection to the Divine not as something set apart from others' connections, but rather as existing alongside them. Not "chosen from among the nations" but "brought near to service," to use Kaplan's phrasing. Yet, to complicate matters further, in some ways it is this emerging new shape of Jewish peoplehood that requires us to not merely reject chosenness but to rethink it in ways we have yet to imagine.

So where does all this leave me? I still believe what I was first taught as a child: God doesn't love one group more than another; Jewish religion is not truer or better than other faiths; and I still am not comfortable with the language of chosenness in my prayers. But, in part, thanks to my experience in interfaith work, I now believe that I am tasked as a Jew with engaging with more of my tradition in all its mysterious, beautiful, and sometimes maddening complexity, including the subject of chosenness. Further, I have learned (not just intellectually, but emotionally) over time that other thoughtful and sensitive people might come to different conclusions about the subject of chosenness or other issues close to my heart. As an interfaith educator, I delight in working with non-Jews who are trying to make sense of their traditions in light of the new realities of their communities. And, as a rabbi, I delight in doing this in Jewish settings with our ever more varied and interesting congregations of Jews and fellow travelers.

I love the metaphor of wrestling (so important to Green's interpretation of the community of Israel) in this context. Chosenness is one of those many ideas with which I wrestle, just as Bishop Stendahl wrestled with some Christian beliefs. Chosenness in some of its previous forms would surely be toxic today. But there may be new forms appropriate to our time. The notion of the chosen people is an idea that, radically rethought, may still have its place. I appreciate the interfaith conversation for renewing my inspiration to "not let it go until it blesses me" (see Genesis 32:26).

QUESTIONS FOR REFLECTION/DISCUSSION

1. Arnold Eisen writes that "Chosenness grips us ... through the power of the pictures it presents ... The love of a parent. A place at the center of things. Work that needs doing and awaits us and no one else. Uniqueness. Blessing." Do these "pictures" resonate with you as you think about your own faith and identity?

2. Are there tropes in your tradition that conflict with your understanding of the validity of other paths to God? How do you wrestle with that contradiction?

3. Do you find it is possible to pray using language with which you do not agree? When, if ever, does it become necessary for you to change the words of your prayers?

4. Arthur Green writes, "Today's universal human challenges are so great that the most important question is 'What does it mean to be a human being?'" In this context, what is the continued relevance of boundaries between Jews and non-Jews, or between any religious groups?

FOR FURTHER READING

Arnold Eisen. *The Chosen People in America*. Bloomington: Indiana University Press, 1983.

Arnold Eisen. "Kaplan and Chosenness: A Historical View." *The Reconstructionist* 50, no. 1 (September 1984): 88–92.

Arthur Green. *Radical Judaism: Rethinking God and Tradition*, 120–66. New Haven, CT: Yale University Press, 2010.

Mordecai M. Kaplan. *The Future of the American Jew*, chapter 13. New York: Macmillan, 1948.

Jonathan Sacks. *The Dignity of Difference: How to Avoid the Clash of Civilizations*, chapter 3. London: Bloomsbury Academic, first edition 2002, revised edition 2003.

II

Personal Virtues in Support of
Interreligious Engagement

7

"Be as Gentle as the Reed"

A Rabbinic Tale about Confronting the Other

BURTON L. VISOTZKY

The Babylonian Talmud stands as a monument to a Jewish civilization that flourished in exile. Jews were removed from the Holy Land to Mesopotamia in 586 BCE, and much of the community remained in the Fertile Crescent even after Ezra and Nehemiah led the exiles back to Jerusalem almost a century later. The community that remained apparently grew and developed in its own way in the centuries that followed. What little evidence we have from this period comes from the Hebrew Bible. Following the canonization of the Hebrew Bible, in the early third century CE Jews from Roman Palestine (the Land of Israel) brought their version of Judaism—rabbinic Judaism—to Jewish Babylonia. Rabbinic academies for study developed, succeeded, and, given the comfort and financial well-being of a close-knit community, grew in strength and confidence. One of the results was that by the sixth century CE, over a millennium after their arrival in Babylonia, the rabbinic community edited a massive compendium of their law, lore, and commentary called the Talmud. It became the normative document for the study of Judaism not only in rabbinic Iraq (as the area later came to be called) but also in medieval Europe. Judaism as we know it today is a product of the dialectal discussions of the Babylonian Talmud, its customs, and its laws.

Among its modes of discourse, the Talmud revels in story-telling. Its tales are often about the rabbis who lived in the Land of Israel centuries earlier. Narrative was a key means for developing Jewish identity and ethic, and the legends that the Talmud spins are didactic, teaching readers how to behave or, sometimes, how *not* to behave. These Jewish "Lives of the Saints" are about rabbis who actually lived, but the stories are not authentic biography or history. The tales are pious fiction, teaching morals, ethics, and right relationship to God and humanity.

For example, Rabbi Shimon bar Yohai, whose son appears in the story below, is regularly depicted as arrogant, a man who believes himself to be among the truly righteous in the world. In fact, he is said to count himself and his son among the chosen few destined for heaven. In the Talmud tractate Sukkah (45b) we read, "Rabbi Shimon bar Yohai said, 'I have seen the sons of heaven and they are but few. If there be a thousand, I and my son are among them; if a hundred, I and my son are among them; and if only two, they are I and my son.'" The medieval Talmudic commentator Rashi explains that these "sons of heaven" are they who behold God's very presence. In Talmudic storytelling, no one accuses Rabbi Shimon of humility! Rabbi Shimon and his son both serve as negative paradigms for what can go wrong when a person has become so learned that he forgets how to relate to those around him. The stories of these two rabbis promote the virtues of humility and employ their arrogance as a pedagogical tool to teach proper comportment toward God's creatures.

Once Rabbi Elazar the son of Rabbi Shimon was coming from his master's school in Migdal G'dor riding his donkey along the riverside. He was arrogantly pleased with himself that he had learned so much Torah.

He chanced across a man who appeared exceedingly ugly. That man said, "Peace/Shalom to you, my Rabbi," but Rabbi Elazar did not return his greeting.

Instead he said to him, "Worthless one! How ugly is that man. Perchance are all the citizens of your town as ugly as you?"

The man replied, "I do not know. But go and tell the Artisan Who made me—'What an ugly vessel you have made.'"

When Rabbi Elazar realized he had sinned, he got down from his donkey and prostrated himself before that man. He apologized, "I have insulted you, please forgive me."

Yet the man demurred saying, "I will not forgive you until you go and tell the Artisan Who made me—'What an ugly vessel you have made.'"

The man followed Rabbi Elazar until he reached his own town, whereupon all the folk of the town came out to greet their Rabbi. They said to him "Peace/Shalom to you our Rabbi, Our Rabbi, Our Teacher, Our Teacher!"

That man asked them, "Whom do you call 'Rabbi, Rabbi'?"

They replied, "Him that follows you."

He said, "If this is your Rabbi, may there not be others like him among the Jewish people!"

They asked, "Why do you say that?!"

He related to them what Rabbi Elazar had done to him. They implored him, "Nevertheless, forgive him, for he is a great man of Torah."

He said, "For your sakes I hereby forgive him, so long as he does not keep doing such."

Rabbi Elazar son of Rabbi Shimon immediately entered the academy and expounded, "One should always be as gentle as the reed and be not hard as the cedar! This is why the reed has the merit to have a pen made from it, with which we write a Torah, phylacteries, and *mezuzahs*."[1]

—Babylonian Talmud, *Taanit* 20a–b

I am taken by how well this religious document grasps the dangers of arrogance and the fact that learning cannot replace proper behavior. Rabbi Elazar learned so much Torah and apparently missed the entire point, that human decency is the goal of God's instruction. As the medieval rabbis regularly formulate it, "Decency takes precedence over Torah." Jews are constantly reminded to see that every human being is created in God's image and likeness (Genesis 1:27). In fact, the Mishnah, the earliest rabbinic document and a compendium of rabbis' legal opinions, waxes somewhat poetic when it comments on the creation of the first human, "Adam was created alone...to teach the ways of peace among God's creatures; so that no one could say to his fellow, 'My father is greater than yours'" (Mishnah *Sanhedrin* 4:5).

---

1. The Torah is the Five Books of Moses, the quintessential document of God's revelation for rabbinic Jews. Phylacteries and *mezuzah*s are the amulets cum mnemonics that the Torah prescribes in Deuteronomy 6:4–9: "Take to heart these instructions...bind them as a sign upon your hand and make them a totem on your forehead (phylacteries); inscribe them on the doorposts (*mezuzah*s) of your house and on your gates."

The Babylonian Talmud looks back on this tale of an ancient Palestinian rabbi from a perceptive distance. The empathy of the exile demands that an arrogant rabbi understand what it means to be seen as the ugly other. The man in the tale is described as exceedingly ugly. At the same time, the man knows his self-worth—just like Rabbi Elazar, he is created by God, in the very image and likeness of the Creator. How clever of our narrator to see both the point of view of the rabbi as well as that of his antagonist. Here is the lesson the editors of the Talmud want us to learn by beginning their telling of the tale from Rabbi Elazar's point of view: *every human being has worth.* Yet when we are too puffed up by our own worth, we may demean others and raise ourselves at the expense of others. We may humiliate and demonize the other. Indeed, we have all too strong a tendency to see those who are not like us as ugly.

The ugly man in our story must be understood as any person debased by another. The debased person might be of a different race. He might be from a different country. He may follow a different religion. He may simply attend a different synagogue, church, or mosque. He may have attended a different university or he may root for a different football team. In our pride and arrogance, we are masterful at seeing those who are not like us as exceedingly ugly. And so, we are caught short when we are reminded that every human being shares the same worth. All of us, no matter what religious path we follow, are vessels fashioned by the same divine Artisan, created in the very image and likeness of the divine Creator. This is true no matter how we worship the Creator. All of us merit the recognition of our relationship with God.

The story also makes clear that leaders, esteemed by their followers, can too easily be guilty of the sin of arrogance. It is not enough for Rabbi Elazar to apologize to or even bow down before the man whom he insulted. The debased man understands that arrogance and superciliousness in a leader must be exposed to those who hold the leader in esteem. When he finally forgives Rabbi Elazar, it is not for the sake of his Torah, for it is clear to the man and to us as readers that Elazar has not learned the lesson taught by the Torah. Rather, the man forgives Elazar for the sake of his townsfolk, the benighted disciples who look up to him. The "ugly" man is the true teacher as he stipulates to Elazar and his community that the rabbi must repent: "I forgive him, so long as he does not keep doing such." To sin is human. To sin and then not repeat the sin is true repentance.

The story ends with an Aesop-like moral from the lips of Rabbi Elazar himself: "Be as gentle as the reed and be not hard as the cedar." The reed is pliable. It bends with the wind and does not snap when pushed. The reed is gentle and, unlike a pen made from hardwood, cannot injure another. The cedar may be a mighty tree, but it is an unfit implement for writing a sacred text. According to this rabbinic teaching, the act of inscribing the text teaches the very lesson inscribed—the medium is the message. The gentleness of the reed makes it appropriate for writing a Torah scroll, phylacteries, or *mezuzah*s, daily reminders for Jews to walk in God's ways. Our story, a tale of an arrogant rabbi on a journey, pointedly reminds us that even learning copious amounts of Torah is no guarantee of staying on the proper path.

Jews are commanded to have physical symbols to remind them of their obligations to God. But the tendency to forget those obligations—to see the other as ugly—is so strong that this rabbinic story suggests one more step in the reminder process. Even as you write the reminder, the very implement of inscription must embody the point: "Be as gentle as the reed, and be not hard as the cedar." It is as much as to say, "Become the very pen that writes the commandment to love the other as yourself. Inscribe upon your heart this commandment, that you might always walk in God's ways and recognize the worth of every creature."

QUESTIONS FOR REFLECTION/DISCUSSION

1. How is the relationship between study and action described in this story?

2. Why was the so-called ugly person so unforgiving? The rabbi, after all, had privately humiliated him; while the "ugly person" publicly humiliated the rabbi. Whose is the greater sin?

3. What might we learn from this story about our relationships with other human beings—within and beyond our religious communities—and with God?

FOR FURTHER READING

Silvina Chemin and Francisco Canzani. *A Dialogue of Life: Towards the Encounter of Jews and Christians.* Hyde Park, NY: New City Press, 2015.

Burton Visotzky and David E. Fishman, eds. *From Mesopotamia to Modernity: Ten Introductions to Jewish History and Literature.* Boulder, CO: Westview Press, 1999.

Kim Zeitman and Mohamed Elsanousi, eds. *Sharing the Well: A Resource Guide for Jewish-Muslim Engagement.* Jewish Theological Seminary, Hartford Seminary, Islamic Society of North America, 2014.

8

"Just as I Have Loved You"

A Christian Hermeneutic of Love as a Resource for Interfaith Engagement

JENNIFER HOWE PEACE

The Gospels of Matthew, Mark, Luke, and John, constitute the first four books of the twenty-seven books of the New Testament. The Gospels were written down within the first century following the death of Jesus, with the scholarly consensus being that Mark was written first, sometime around 70 CE while Matthew and Luke were likely composed separately between 80 and 90 CE. Scholars consider the Gospel of John, distinct in style and content from the first three, to have been written by about 90 or 100 CE.

Matthew, Mark, and Luke are often considered in parallel and referred to as the "Synoptic Gospels." They include many of the same stories about Jesus in roughly the same order.[1] However, each of the four Gospels presents a slightly distinct perspective on and portrait of the life, ministry, death, and resurrection of Jesus. Unlike contemporary historical-biographical writing, the Gospels (literally, "Good News") were written to be more than just a

---

1. There are many books that introduce readers to the Gospels. One book that presents Gospel passages side by side is: Burton H. Throckmorton Jr., *Gospel Parallels: A Comparison of the Synoptic Gospels, New Revised Standard Version*, 5th rev. ed. (Nashville: Thomas Nelson, 1992).

record of Jesus' life. They played a role in shoring up early Christian identity, differentiating Christianity from other religious groups, and inspiring others to join the Christian community.

While individual Christians and denominational bodies differ in terms of the degree of authority granted to the Bible, it continues to be a central source for Christian theology, ethics, and identity. I relate to the Bible as a rich repository of revelations from and about God. It chronicles an unfolding understanding of the nature and meaning of the Divine-human relationship. While the Bible is not the sole or sufficient authority of my faith, I consider it a central and "living text" that still speaks to me.

Matthew: 22:36–39[2]
"Teacher, which commandment in the law is the greatest?" He said to him, "You shall love the Lord your God with all your heart, and with all your soul, and with all your mind. This is the greatest and first commandment. And a second is like it: You shall love your neighbor as yourself. On these two commandments hang all the law and the prophets."

Mark 12:28–31
One of the scribes came near and heard them disputing with one another, and seeing that he answered them well, he asked him, "Which commandment is the first of all?" Jesus answered, "The first is 'Hear, O Israel, the Lord our God, the Lord is one; you shall love the Lord your God with all your heart, and with all your soul and with all your mind, and with all your strength.' The second is this, 'You shall love your neighbor as yourself.' There is no other commandment greater than these."

2. All biblical quotes are from the New Revised Standard Version.

Luke 10:25–28

Just then a lawyer stood up to test Jesus. "Teacher," he said, "what must I do to inherit eternal life?" He said to him, "What is written in the law? What do you read there?" He answered, "You shall love the Lord your God with all your heart, and with all your soul, and with all your strength, and with all your mind; and your neighbor as yourself." And he said to him, "You have given the right answer; do this and you will live."

John 13:34–35

"I give you a new commandment, that you love one another. Just as I have loved you, you also should love one another. By this everyone will know that you are my disciples, if you have love for one another."

"How many of us have given up trying to convert our spouses, parents, children, friends to think and believe exactly like we do without that lessening the love we feel for them?" I posed this question to a group of fellow academics and administrators at a neighboring university. One participant nodded and shared a story in response. An Evangelical Christian, he was taken aback when as a freshman in college he discovered that his roommate was a devout Muslim. Despite his initial apprehension, he described the respect and friendship that grew between them over the course of the year. Now, decades after graduating, they remained close friends. "We disagree on just about everything that matters to us," he said, "but I love him."

Love is a profound and remarkable resource for interfaith work. It often clusters with a whole host of other dispositions that enable authentic engagement across lines of difference: humility, curiosity, forgiveness, and hope to name a few. It allows us to say, as this story illustrates, "I may not agree with you, but I love you so I'm listening."

Both my personal experiences and my understanding of the Gospel passages cited above lead me to assume a posture of love when approaching both religious "others" and Christian scripture.[3] In fact, a *hermeneutic of love* has become my primary interpretive tool for understanding how to translate the meaning of a sacred text into an obligation of my faith.[4] "If God's purpose is Love, then what is required of me?" This is the refrain I carry. If a particular passage seems to contradict this orienting assertion, I assume I need to work harder to glean a faithful understanding of

---

3. The emphasis on using the commandment to love God and neighbor as an interpretive key for understanding the whole of scripture has a long history. Augustine of Hippo, a fourth-century Christian bishop and church father, writes about using a principle of *charity* in interpreting the Bible. "According to Augustine, the ultimate purpose of biblical edification is to lead man [*sic*] to the greater love of God and the other. Therefore, this overarching concern of the Biblical message serves as the hermeneutic key to understanding the Bible. When a literal understanding of Scripture should be propounded, and when a figurative understanding of Scripture should be adopted, depends on the application of this hermeneutic rule. The better interpretation is that which will lead to the greater love of God and the other." Alon Goshen Gottstein, "Love as a Hermeneutic Principle in Rabbinic Literature," *Journal of Literature & Theology* 8, no. 3 (September 1994): 262, accessed at http://www.elijah-interfaith.org/uploads/media/love_hermeneutic_principle.pdf on March 31, 2015. In this essay, Gottstein is contrasting "Augustine's principle of charity in interpreting the Bible" (from *On Christian Doctrine* III.x) with Rabbi Avika's "hermeneutic of love," which emphasizes God's love for humankind rather than human love for God.

4. While this particular articulation and application of a "hermeneutic of love" is my own, other interreligious scholars have used this term in various ways. For example, Werner Jeanrond uses the term more broadly and proposes "co-developing a critical hermeneutics of love," adding that "[s]uch an interdisciplinary hermeneutics acknowledges the basic communicative relationality of human beings. It approaches both the phenomenon of religion and the particularity of religious traditions from the perspective of their potential to form communities of respect, mutual engagement and openness toward transcendence and transformation." Werner Jeanrond, "Toward an Interreligious Hermeneutics of Love," in *Interreligious Hermeneutics*, ed. Catherine Cornille and Christopher Conway (Eugene, OR: Cascade Books), 59. See also Oddbjørn Leirvik, *Interreligious Studies: A Relational Approach to Religious Activism and the Study of Religion* (London: Bloomsbury, 2014).

the text and its implications. I turn to various inductive and deductive tools (prayer, reflection, historical-critical interpretations, and insights from various scholars and practitioners, past and present).[5]

In the passages from Matthew, Mark, and Luke, Jesus, in good rabbinic fashion, is creatively engaging with Hebrew scripture in conversation with fellow Jews.[6] From Deuteronomy 6:3–5, he quotes, "Hear, O Israel: The Lord is our God, the Lord alone.[7] You shall love the Lord your God with all your heart, and with all your soul, and with all your might." Jesus links this commandment with another commandment from Leviticus 19:18: "... you shall love your neighbor as yourself."

In a passage distinct to Luke's Gospel, the lawyer who engaged Jesus in conversation asks a follow-up question: "And who is my neighbor?"[8] Jesus responds with the parable of the

---

5. For example, fourteenth-century theologian, mystic, and English anchoress Julian of Norwich writes about Love as God's purpose in her *Revelations of Divine Love*. "And from the time that [the vision] was shown, I desired often to know what our Lord's meaning was. And fifteen years and more afterward I was answered in my spiritual understanding, thus: 'Would you know your Lord's meaning in this thing? Know it well, love was his meaning. Who showed it to you? Love. What did he show you? Love. Why did he show it? For love. Keep yourself therein and you shall know and understand more in the same. But you shall never know nor understand any other thing, forever. Thus I was taught that love was our Lord's meaning. And I saw quite clearly in this and in all, that before God made us, he loved us, which love was never slaked nor ever shall be." *Julian of Norwich: Showings*, Classics of Western Spirituality (New York: Paulist Press, 1977), 342–43.

6. For an excellent exploration of the importance and relevance of understanding Jesus as a first-century Jew, see Amy Jill Levine's *The Misunderstood Jew: The Church and the Scandal of the Jewish Jesus* (New York: HarperOne, 2007) and James Carroll's *Christ Actually: The Son of God for the Secular Age* (New York: Viking, 2014).

7. This first sentence, referred to only in Mark's account, is called the "*Sh'ma*" in Judaism. It is a key theological and devotional text that is traditionally included in Jewish daily prayer services (morning and evening) and at other times.

8. The "lawyer" refers here to an expert in Jewish law and lore (including the TaNaKh). So, this encounter is perhaps less like a defense attorney cross-examining Jesus and more like an esteemed theology professor testing the brash new teacher in town.

Good Samaritan: "A man was going down from Jerusalem to Jericho, and fell into the hands of robbers..."[9] What strikes me about this popular Christian parable about the virtues of helping others is that the answer to the lawyer's question, "Who is my neighbor?" has nothing to do with the religious, ethnic, or economic identity of the injured traveler, but is defined by the actions and attitudes of the protagonist. The question Jesus' parable really addresses is not "Who is my neighbor?" but rather "Am I acting like a neighbor?"

"Which of these three, do you think, was a neighbor to the man who fell into the hands of the robbers?" Jesus asks the lawyer.

"The one who showed him mercy," says the lawyer.

"Go and do likewise," Jesus responds.

To be a neighbor is to show mercy. The question "Who is my neighbor?" cannot be answered with words alone, but must be accompanied by right actions. Being a neighbor is not a passive state. Being a neighbor is a decision we make, an attitude we adopt, and actions we take. It is also worth noting that, in this parable, loving one's neighbor and showing mercy are not conflated with conversion. The healed traveler and the Samaritan part ways with their identities intact.

---

9. The full text of this parable is as follows: "A man was going down from Jerusalem to Jericho, and fell into the hands of robbers, who stripped him, beat him, and went away, leaving him half dead. Now by chance a priest was going down that road; and when he saw him, he passed by on the other side. So likewise a Levite, when he came to the place and saw him, passed by on the other side. But a Samaritan while traveling came near him; and when he saw him, he was moved with pity. He went to him and bandaged his wounds, having poured oil and wine on them. Then he put him on his own animal and brought him to an inn, and took care of him. The next day he took out two denarii, gave them to the innkeeper, and said, 'Take care of him; and when I come back, I will repay you whatever more you spend.' Which of these three, do you think, was a neighbor to the man who fell into the hands of the robbers?" He said, "the one who showed him mercy." Jesus said to him, "Go and do likewise."

Reading the four Gospels together, the passage from John offers what Jesus calls "a new commandment," and adds a slight twist to our understanding of the Great Commandment: "Just as I have loved you, you also should love one another." The dependent clause in this statement suggests that our capacity for love comes from and is modeled on Jesus' love for his disciples, God's love for God's people.

As we move closer to God, we are better able to mirror God's compassion and expand our capacity to love others (adding ourselves to the mix here complicates the argument). This does not only apply to our close friends and family. A wider sense of God's unconditional love for each of us invites us to extend our love to those who we might otherwise think of as unlovable, unworthy, or even "the enemy." As Jesus says, "Love your enemies, do good to those who hate you, bless those who curse you, pray for those who abuse you" (Luke 6:27).[10]

If we are to love as God has loved us, we need to ask about the nature of God's love for us. Scripture offers many parables and passages that focus on the meaning of love, from the "love is

---

10. The subject of loving one's enemies could easily generate a whole separate essay and has been the focus of countless past Christian reflections. One orientation I find helpful comes from Beverly Wildung Harrison, a Christian ethicist and feminist theologian who writes: "We live in a time when massive and accumulated injustice, acted out over time, encounters answers in the rising anger of those whose dignity and life are being threatened by collective patterns of privilege that have to be undone. In a world such as this, actively pursuing the works of love will often mean doing all we can to stop the crucifixions, resisting the evil as best we can, or mitigating the suffering of those who are the victims of our humanly disordered relations. In the midst of such a world, it is still within the power of love, which is the good news of God, to keep us in the knowledge that none of us were born only to die, that we were meant to have the gift of life, to know the power of relation and to pass it on." See Harrison's essay, "The Power of Anger in the Work of Love," in *Weaving the Visions: New Patterns in Feminist Spirituality*, ed. Judith Plaskow and Carol Christ (San Francisco: HarperOne, 1989), 214–25.

patient, love is kind" portrait of virtues in 1 Corinthians 13:4–13 to the parable of the Good Samaritan which emphasizes love as just action. The quest to understand what it means to love one's enemies, to experience and reflect God's love for us in our encounters with others, is at the heart of what it means to be a Christian.

Beyond scripture, I see this quest reflected in the lives of people like Father Gregory Boyle, a Jesuit priest who has worked with gang members in Los Angeles for the last twenty-five years. He founded an organization called "Homeboy Industries" that puts enemies from rival gangs to work side by side. As he notes, "Human beings can't demonize people they know. It's hard to sustain that." Similarly, the first task of interfaith work is humanizing the "other" through the slow, steady, side-by-side work of relationship-building reflected in programs like this one.

Father Boyle links his work in the world to his understanding of a loving God: "If you presume that God is compassionate loving-kindness, all we're asked to do is to be in the world who God is. You're always trying to imitate the kind of God you believe in. You want to move away from whatever is tiny-spirited and judgmental. You want to be as spacious as you can be."[11] In Father Boyle's logic, the deeper my connection to God's expansive love, the more capable I will be of manifesting this in my relations with others. This is also Jesus' logic in linking the two parts of the Great Commandment: loving God "with all your heart, and with all your soul, and with all your strength, and with all your mind; and your neighbor as yourself." My own commitment to this

---

11. "The Calling of Delight: Gangs, Service and Kinship," Father Gregory Boyle interviewed by Krista Tippett, *OnBeing*, April 2, 2015, http://www.onbeing.org/program/father-greg-boyle-on-the-calling-of-delight/5053.

inseparable link is reflected in the dual areas of my teaching, Christian spirituality and interfaith studies, each of which is an expression of and a way to live out the other.

A *hermeneutic of love* is a profound resource for Christians engaged in interfaith work. It can guide engagements with both scripture and the world as we embody the kind of God we believe in. In this sense, interfaith work is not inconsistent with or even tangential to being Christian but is in fact a significant *way of being Christian*.[12] As we expand our own capacity to love we extend with ever-greater generosity our understanding of what it means to be neighbors to each other.

QUESTIONS FOR REFLECTION/DISCUSSION

1. What is the place of love in your religious or ethical worldview? How does one create or cultivate a disposition of love?

2. What do you think of the assertion that interfaith engagement is a "way of being Christian" (or a way of being a devotee of another spiritual path)?

3. To what extent does being a faithful or committed member of your own religious or ethical tradition support or enhance your commitment to interreligious engagement?

---

12. Mark Heim, professor of theology at Andover Newton Theological School, described interfaith engagement as a "way of being Christian" during a panel discussion at Andover Newton about religious pluralism. For related comments, see Heim's essay, "The Shifting Significance of Theologies of Religious Pluralism," in *Understanding Religious Pluralism: Perspectives from Religious Studies and Theology*, ed. Peter C. Phan and Jonathan S. Ray (Eugene, OR: Pickwick Publications, 2014), 242–59.

FOR FURTHER READING

James Carroll. *Christ Actually: The Son of God for the Secular Age*. New York: Viking, 2014.

Alon Goshen Gottstein. "Love as a Hermeneutic Principle in Rabbinic Literature." *Journal of Literature & Theology* 8, no. 3 (September 1994): 248–67.

Mark Heim. "The Shifting Significance of Theologies of Religious Pluralism." In *Understanding Religious Pluralism: Perspectives from Religious Studies and Theology*, edited by Peter C. Phan and Jonathan S. Ray, 249–59. Eugene, OR: Pickwick Publications, 2014.

Julian of Norwich: Showings, Classics of Western Spirituality. Translated by Edmund Colledge and James Walsh. New York: Paulist Press, 1977.

Amy Jill Levine. *The Misunderstood Jew: The Church and the Scandal of the Jewish Jesus*. New York: HarperOne, 2007.

Burton H. Throckmorton, Jr. *Gospel Parallels: A Comparison of the Synoptic Gospels, New Revised Standard Version*. 5th rev. ed. Nashville: Thomas Nelson, 1992.

9

Sūrah al-ʿAlaq
and Dispositions for Interreligious Engagement

CELENE IBRAHIM

The Qur'an is traditionally understood by Muslims to be a message to all humankind from God.[1] The Qur'an, literally "recitation," is said to have been delivered through the Archangel Gabriel (*Jibrīl*)[2] to the Messenger of God.[3] The Qur'an describes itself as originating from the same source as other divine messages,[4] including scriptures given to Jesus (*ʿĪsā*), David (*Dāʾūd*), and Moses (*Mūsā*). The Qur'an has 114 segments (s. *surah*, pl. *suwar*) consisting of a given number of verses or "signs" (s. *ayah*, pl. *ayāt*). These "signs" often directly relate to specific incidents and personalities, but more universal meanings are contained within the particulars.

With regard to *Sūrah al-ʿAlaq* below, there is near unanimous agreement among Muslim scholars that verses 1–5 are the

---

1. The Qur'anic understanding of God is in some ways similar to but in other ways different from the conception of God in other faiths; I use God/Allah to reflect both the similarity and the particularity. For a rich introduction to God in the Islamic intellectual tradition, see the Nawawi Foundation lectures by Hamza Yusuf and Umar Abd-Allah, "The Attributes of God in Islam" (Chicago: Alhambra Productions, 2004).

2. It is customary in Islamic contexts to recite short blessings and supplications whenever the name of an archangel, messenger, prophet, or esteemed person is mentioned.

3. It is customary in Islamic contexts to avoid using the proper name of Muhammad (c. 570–632 CE) out of reverence. Out of respect, an epithet such as "Messenger of God" is commonly used when speaking about the Prophet Muhammad.

4. This source is referred to in the Qur'an as the "preserved tablet" (*al-lawḥ al-maḥfūẓ*, e.g., Q. 85:22) or "mother of the book" (*umm al-kitāb*, e.g., Q. 13:39).

very first that the Archangel *Jibrīl* brought to the Messenger of God. According to Muslim accounts, the other verses of this section were brought by *Jibrīl* in a later year. These verses are both the Messenger's call to prophethood and a reminder of the centrality of both learning and humility in Islam. The remaining verses of this surah come in response to altercations that the Messenger had with his tribesman, nicknamed by the Muslims Abū Jahl (lit. "Father of Ignorance"), who continually insulted and physically harassed the Messenger. In this sense, the verses provide an example for how to uphold righteous conduct when faced with bigotry and harassment.

While the selection below is perhaps not an obvious interreligious resource, upon closer examination, this surah provides readers of the Qur'an with several key insights for interreligious engagement.

SŪRAH AL-'ALAQ (96)

1) Recite in the Name of thy Master Who created;

2) created the human from a clinging clot.

3) Recite! Thy Master is the Most Generous/Noble/Bountiful.[5]

4) Who taught by the Pen,

5) taught the human what s/he[6] did not know.

6) Nay, truly the human exceeds all bounds,

7) when s/he considers her/himself as self-sufficient.

---

5. I have included several alternate translations to give English readers a fuller sense of the Arabic meanings.

6. The singular pronoun in Arabic can be inclusive of both genders; as English does not have such a pronoun, s/he is used here.

8) Truly unto your Master is the return.

9) Have you seen he who prohibits

10) a slave when he prays?

11) Have you seen if he is upon guidance,

12) or bidding to God-wariness?

13) Have you seen when he rejects and turns away?

14) Does he not know that God sees?

15) Nay! If he does not stop, We [God] shall seize him
    by the forelock,[7]

16) a lying, iniquitous forelock.

17) So let him summon his cohorts!

18) We [God] shall summon the keepers of Hell.

19) Nay! Heed him not, but prostrate and draw near.[8]

There are many different goals, methods, and formats for interreligious engagement. The goals may be to coordinate social services, to affect policy, or to improve the wellbeing of a given group. Interreligious engagement may be motivated by curiosity or by a personal quest for meaning, truth, knowledge, connection, and community. The aim of interreligious engagement may be to inspire transformation of hearts, intellects, and attitudes, or to effect change within policy, systems, or social structures. Apart

---

7. Both the first person (singular and plural) and the third person can refer to God/Allah in the Qur'an.

8. This is a verse of prostration where it is customary to pause in the recitation in order to perform a posture of *sujūd* with forehead, nose, hands, knees, and toes touching the floor and head pointed in the direction of the Ka'ba sanctuary in Mecca.

from its particular motivations, interreligious engagement requires specific dispositions, certain interpersonal skills, and a unique willingness on the part of the individuals involved to navigate irreducibly different worldviews and value systems. Here I highlight three ways in which *Sūrah al-'Alaq* calls attention to some of the "best practices" that I have found helpful for this engagement.

Cultivating Humility and Wisdom through Knowledge and Prayer
Much of the Qur'an, including *Sūrah al-'Alaq*, includes an exhortation of one kind or another to seek out and benefit from knowledge. This surah suggests that, despite God having bestowed writing as a unique capacity and generous gift to humans (vv. 3–5), people will resist new learning if a sense of self-sufficiency dominates over the recognition of human interdependency and dependency on an ultimate Power (vv. 7–8). As if to emphasize this need for profound humility and growth, this surah begins by calling attention to the lowly origins of the human being as a clinging clot (v. 2), a clot that is remarkably transformed into a creature capable of intellection.

In the next few lines, the ideal of humility and engagement with transformative learning is contrasted with an example of human ignorance and arrogance (vv. 9–11). The All-Seeing One then promises to seize the arrogant, ignorant, and troublesome one by the forelock (vv. 14–16). Grabbing by the forelock is a action done to gain control over a herd animal, suggesting that the one who does not benefit from recitation, reading, writing, and learning, when it is readily available, is akin to a creature without the capacity for higher levels of reason: "They are like livestock; nay, they are even more astray" (Q. 7:179). The forelock is also of significance because it is immediately adjacent to the precise location of the brain's capacity for reason and logical reflection. It is also the part of the head that is placed on the ground in prostration during ritual prayer, as alluded to in this surah (v. 19) and as performed by devout Muslims when they recite or hear this verse.[9]

For me, these verses are a reminder that humility is a mark of wisdom and that one of the results of diligent prayer, in its many forms, is the cultivation of humility. Here, humility is both a prerequisite to engaging in learning (epitomized in verse 5) and a direct result of the learning (epitomized in verse 19). *Sūrah al-ʿAlaq* states that humble engagement with transformative learning is the unique purpose of the human species. At its best, interreligious engagement presents opportunities to humbly engage with ancient wisdom traditions, time-honored forms of prayer, and the ruminations of inspired persons throughout the ages.

On a related point, the surah also calls attention to the importance of entire bodily submission and acts of ritual devotion in the process of acquiring wisdom. As the Messenger is reported to have said: "The length of a person's prayer and the shortness of his sermons are a sign of understanding. So, prolong prayer and shorten sermons…"[10] There is a lesson here too for interreligious engagement. Often interreligious gatherings turn into panel sessions or heady debates, and while such forms of encounter have their place and purpose, I have personally found that some of the most powerful moments in interreligious encounter come from simply and humbly witnessing another person's sincerity and humility in prayer or in mindful practice.

Dignity and Patient Perseverance when Confronted with Religious Bigotry

In addition to commending the disposition of profound humility, *Sūrah al-ʿAlaq* contains an important description of patience,

---

9. See note 8 above.

10. As reported by ʿAmār bin Yāsir. Adapted from the compilation by Charles Le Gai Eaton, *The Book of Hadith: Sayings of the Prophet Muhammad, from the Mishkat al-Masabih* (Watsonville, CA: The Book Foundation, 2008), 34.

perseverance, and piety in the face of bigotry. The capacity for patient perseverance is extremely relevant for fruitful civic interreligious work, particularly when it has become somewhat of a sport for each group to push the boundaries of civility and come up with the vilest and most widely circulated libel and slander about the other. In this context, the persona of the Prophet Muhammad is regularly defamed by persons and groups specifically aiming to offend and provoke. The Messenger, in fact, faced much ridicule and persecution during his lifetime, and abundant reports from the earliest generations of Muslims describe his patient perseverance in the face of taunting and acts of ill will aimed at undermining his dignity, personhood, and message. In *Sūrah al-'Alaq,* the Messenger is directly commanded to not heed the provocation, but instead to draw near to God through prostration (v. 19). In another Qur'anic verse, the Messenger, and Muslims at large, are commanded to counteract evil deeds by beautiful deeds such that interpersonal relationships may become transformative: "Repel [the evil deeds] with that which is better, then behold, the one between whom and thee there is enmity shall be as if he were a loyal protecting friend" (Q. 41:34). The Qur'an does not mince words when it comes to the most pious and best way to respond to ridicule: "The servants of the Most Merciful are those who walk upon the earth gently, and when the ignorant address them, they reply with words of peace" (Q. 25:36).

It is likely that at some point a person seeking to build interreligious connection will face ridicule and persecution, whether overt or subtle. *Sūrah al-'Alaq* provides strong encouragement to maintain piety and a good demeanor. On a related note, individuals who carry out heinous crimes while claiming to defend the dignity of the Messenger do not follow his own example. Despite the fact that this is well known within the Muslim contexts that I am a part of, I have found this an important message to reiterate in interreligious contexts where there may be confusion over Islamic tenets. The Messenger is known as "a mercy to all humankind," and he elevated the rights to life, property, dignity, honor, and bodily integrity for all people, not just those who were self-professed Muslims.

Striving to Appreciate Particularity and Nuance When Engaging Difference

In no uncertain language, in *Sūrah al-'Alaq* God vows to intervene on behalf of the Messenger against those who persecute him (vv. 14–18). Particularly in contexts that are rife with stereotypes of Muslims as violent and fanatical, Qur'anic verses (such as vv. 15–18 above) speaking about God's vengeance, God's punishments, and Hell could be taken to reinforce perceptions and stereotypes of Muslims as prone to vengeance. When engaging interreligously, it is indispensable to appreciate the particulars that distinguish religions and strive to understand how the particulars relate to create a meaningful conceptual system. For instance, the concept of God's punishment for wrongdoers is indeed core to Islamic teachings, but God's benevolence, forgiveness, and mercy are arguably even more pivotal throughout the Qur'an and teachings of the Messenger. The Qur'an proclaims that: "God has inscribed upon Godself mercy" (Q. 6:12), and promises goodness for all those who believe, do righteous works, and enjoin justice and perseverance (Q. 103).

The Qur'an describes its message as containing both good news and warning (e.g., Q. 33:45), and devout Muslims are instructed to simultaneously maintain both hope for God's mercy and fear of God's wrath. God, as described in the Qur'an, has qualities of might and majesty as well as gentleness and compassion. God is the One who Abases (*al-khāfiḍ*) and the One who Raises in Rank (*al-rāfi'*), the One who Humiliates (*al-mudhill*) and the One who Bestows Honor *(al-mu'izz)*, the Reckoner *(al-muntaqim)* and the Pardoner *(al-'afuww)*, the Bearer of Harm *(al-dārr)* and the One who Averts Harm *(al-māni')*. All of these qualities and attributes of God and more are reflected in *Sūrah al-'Alaq* above.

Perhaps in recognition of the fact that humans are motivated by both the promise of reward and the threat of punishment, the Qur'an contains plentiful and vivid imagery of hellfire and punishment for the unremorseful.

The Qur'an describes a God who regularly intervenes in human affairs, who judges, and who assigns destinies. At the same time, it stresses that the only distinction of relevance that God "sees" between people is piety (e.g., Q. 2:177)—not ethnicity, genealogy, birthplace, wealth, sect, or any other factor. This current life is described as a testing ground of each individual's morality, character, and obedience to God's command. In light of this test of life, human beings are encouraged to cultivate God-wariness through religious learning, observation of the physical universe, and acts of worship to the One.

Often in organized interreligious gatherings, the similarities between faith traditions—such as virtues of compassion or ethical imperatives for caring for the poor—are put on display without due appreciation of the important or uncomfortable particularities, such as notions of God's wrath, judgment, and Hell, that make religious scriptures, practices, and beliefs distinct, nuanced, and meaningful. I have found that some interfaith initiatives miss out on opportunities to build resilient relationships because the format does not allow sufficient space and time for participants to communicate intimately about their irreducible differences. On one occasion the Qur'an instructs: "Invite to the way of your Lord with wisdom and good instruction, and debate with them in a way that is best..." (Q. 16:125).

When encountering irreducible differences, I have learned to apply a hermeneutic of generosity and engage holistically. Holistic and robust interreligious engagement requires surrendering the impulse to seek consensus and instead request being open to engaging with and weighing differing truth claims, perspectives, understandings, and worldviews. This sphere of engagement invites such disagreement that humility, the concept with which I began, is an absolute prerequisite. It also requires a certain patient perseverance, both with one's own learning process and the ignorance, willful or innocent, of others. Benefiting from interreligious encounter requires, among other things, the ability to detect prejudices, dispel faulty preconceived notions, suspend mistrust, and possibly even change one's views and opinions, if only momentarily, in an effort to empathize with another's experience.

In the hope of expanding the resources for interreligious engagement, I have selected verses of the Qur'an above that are not often the ones chosen for interfaith programs. I have highlighted the value of humility in the pursuit of knowledge, the need for patient perseverance in the face of bigotry, and the necessity to engage the particulars of different belief systems with a generous hermeneutic and holistic eye for how the particulars become meaningful.

To learn from the Islamic intellectual heritage, and to collaborate alongside Muslims in civic activism, it is important to make and attempt to robustly engage with the texts and ideas that Muslims hold dear, even—and perhaps most especially—when they present different perspectives on divinity and humanity. The Qur'an says that "there is no compulsion in faith" (2:256), and that humankind was made into nations and tribes such that we may know one another (Q. 49:13). The Qur'an describes humans as all descending from a single soul (Q. 4:1). Even the diversity of religious traditions in the world is described as part of divine intent (e.g. Q. 10:99). Different communities are instructed to "vie with one another in good works" (Q. 2:148) in a spirit of generosity and mutual recognition of human dignity.[11] May it be so.

QUESTIONS FOR REFLECTION/DISCUSSION

1. What is the role of speech, writing, learning, and intellect in these verses?

2. How do you understand "the return" in verse eight of this passage?

3. What are the implications of a scripture that depicts itself variously as guidance, warning, wisdom, good news, a sign, a reminder, a criterion, a clear explanation, a decisive word, revelation, and the speech of the divine? How are these qualities similar to or different from other scriptures? Do you see these qualities reflected in the verses above?

4. Have you ever faced religious bigotry or persecution? If so, how did you respond? Where did you find solace?

---

11. This is a brief account and does not take into consideration the full range and levels of meanings of *Sūrah al-ʿAlaq*. Further study of these Qur'anic verses and principles mentioned here would look at parallels and resonances with other places in the Qur'an and within the extensive collections of the teachings and insights from the life of the Messenger. Furthermore, the Qur'an is first and foremost an aural experience, and when recited the verses have a unique consonance, assonance, rhythm, and tone. Readers are encouraged to explore the resource section to encounter these aural dimensions that cannot be captured in writing and in translation. In fact, the Qur'an is only the Arabic Qur'an; a translation into any other language is an approximation and interpretation.

FOR FURTHER READING

Charles Le Gai Eaton. *The Book of Hadith: Sayings of the Prophet Muhammad, from the Mishkat al-Masabih*. Watsonville, CA: The Book Foundation, 2008.

Carl Ernst. *How to Read the Qur'an: A New Guide, with Select Translations*. Chapel Hill: University of North Carolina Press, 2011.

Ingrid Mattson. *The Story of the Qur'an: Its History and Place in Muslim Life*. 2nd ed. Malden, MA: John Wiley & Sons, Ltd., 2013.

'Alī Qulī Qarā'ī, trans. *The Qur'an: With a Phrase-by-Phrase English Translation*. London: Islamic College for Advanced Studies Press, 2004.

Michael Sells. *Approaching the Qur'an: The Early Revelations*. 2nd ed. Ashland, OR: White Cloud Press, 2006.

Hazma Yusuf and Umar Abd-Allah. "The Attributes of God in Islam." Audio lectures. Chicago: Alhambra Productions, 2004.

10

Hospitality, Communal Responsibility, and Humility

Secular Humanism and "The New Colossus"

ESTHER BOYD

Not like the brazen giant of Greek fame,
With conquering limbs astride from land to land;
Here at our sea-washed, sunset gates shall stand
A mighty woman with a torch, whose flame
Is the imprisoned lightning, and her name
Mother of Exiles. From her beacon-hand
Glows world-wide welcome; her mild eyes command
The air-bridged harbor that twin cities frame.

"Keep, ancient lands, your storied pomp!" cries she
With silent lips. "Give me your tired, your poor,
Your huddled masses yearning to breathe free,
The wretched refuse of your teeming shore.
Send these, the homeless, tempest-tost to me,
I lift my lamp beside the golden door!"

—"The New Colossus" by Emma Lazarus

In the midst of a period of intense public debate about issues of identity, civil liberties, and nationalism, I find myself returning to Emma Lazarus's classic poem, "The New Colossus," engraved on the pedestal of the Statue of Liberty.[1] I view it as an affirmation of our purpose and our potential, both as a country and as a global community. Lazarus's words serve as a reminder of what lies at the heart of the democratic project: the idea that all are created equal and deserve freedom and justice.

Emma Lazarus, though not from among the poor, huddled masses herself, wrote extensively and eloquently against anti-Semitism and xenophobia. As a Jewish woman in the mid-nineteenth century, she witnessed the difficulties facing immigrants to the United States, including bigotry, fear, and violence. She experienced firsthand the otherness that was cast over her community, as too many of her fellow Americans turned a blind eye to the terrible suffering of Jews in Eastern Europe at the time.[2] "The New Colossus," is a bold call stretching across the ocean; it is a challenge and a battle cry against those who would look away rather than reach out. The selection of her poem for the Statue of Liberty suggests that her vision of radical hospitality was one that resonated deeply with nineteenth-century Americans. This same ideal continues to resonate with me today, and it dovetails with the ethic of communal responsibility at the heart of the current Humanist Manifesto (III):[3]

---

1. This poem appears in its entirely on a plaque on the inside of the pedestal, and only the section beginning, "Give me your tired..." appears on the outside. Because of this, this poem is rarely quoted in its entirety.

2. To learn more about Emma Lazarus, visit the Jewish Women's Archive, https://jwa.org/womenofvalor/lazarus.

3. The first Humanist Manifesto was penned in 1933 and was written as a description of developing ideas rather than a creed. The original Manifesto was then replaced by the Humanist Manifesto II in 1973, which attempted to grapple with the realities of the past few decades, including World War II, the Vietnam War, and the civil rights and women's liberation movements. Both earlier versions have been replaced by Manifesto III, which was published in 2003. It is expected that this document will continue to be revised and updated to reflect an ethic of humanism that is responsive to reality and driven toward the betterment of the global community. For more information about the Manifesto, its authors, and the different versions, visit the American Humanist Association (http://www.americanhumanist.org).

Humans are social by nature and find meaning in relationships. Humanists long for and strive toward a world of mutual care and concern, free of cruelty and its consequences, where differences are resolved cooperatively without resorting to violence. The joining of individuality with interdependence enriches our lives, encourages us to enrich the lives of others, and inspires hope of attaining peace, justice, and opportunity for all.

Working to benefit society maximizes individual happiness. Progressive cultures have worked to free humanity from the brutalities of mere survival and to reduce suffering, improve society, and develop global community. We seek to minimize the inequities of circumstance and ability, and we support a just distribution of nature's resources and the fruits of human effort so that as many as possible can enjoy a good life.

I first became involved in interfaith work for practical reasons. As a secular humanist and an atheist without a home community, I found that interfaith projects offered me opportunities to work on peace and justice issues I cared about most deeply and to put my values into practice in meaningful ways alongside others who were doing the same. When functioning well, interfaith spaces invite people from different walks of life to bring their particular resources, expertise, and insights forward for the benefit of a wider swath of society. Today, therefore, I understand my interreligious efforts as an expression of my commitment to the core principles in the Humanist Manifesto. That is, the "joining of individuality with interdependence" for the sake of mutual enrichment in pursuit of "peace, justice, and opportunity for all."

Over many years of interfaith work, both personal and professional, I have come to view the spaces we create through interreligious peace and justice efforts as "sacred." While this is not a common term in the secular humanist community, I find it a fitting way to express what feels so powerful about joining with others across lines of difference in an effort to build a more equitable and caring society. Lazarus's summons to the tempest-tossed and weary is an invitation to help fashion such a "space" nationally. In this vision, hospitality and communal responsibility are two interconnected pieces of a whole.

This is, perhaps, why I find "The New Colossus," so striking. The vision, immortalized on the base of a statue that has become an internationally recognized symbol of the United States, demands open access to all, especially those in need. By beckoning the powerless and downtrodden to her shores, the "Mother of Exiles" invites immigrants and refugees to participate in the project of American democracy, to embody the idea that all people "are created equal." This is an idealistic view of immigration policy, to be sure, but even as it remains aspirational, the vision demands that we continue to reach out, to offer succor and sustenance, and to deal compassionately with those in need. This work never was—nor will it ever be—simple. We must continue to discuss and debate ethical and judicial matters rigorously, and to make difficult decisions. It is noteworthy that the Mother of Exiles is *not* a conqueror, but a comforter. Living into this vision is not a means to certain victory. The work is hard, and it is never complete. Our commitments to hospitality and communal responsibility require us to commit to striving, day after day, with others with whom we agree and disagree in our efforts to create the kind of shared civil society we long for.

Reflecting on the values of hospitality and communal responsibility also requires us to carefully consider the place of humility in our peace and justice efforts. Most basically, we must acknowledge that all of our work is partial and incomplete. There will always be more to do. When overwhelmed by this fact, I often find myself repeating Theodore Roosevelt's words in mantra-like fashion, "Do what you can, with what you have, where you are." These simple words remind us that though we are not capable of solving every problem (or every aspect of any problem), we are not excused from doing our part simply because it is small. There is always *something* we can do. It is also a call to create partnerships and coalitions whenever possible as a way of refining our vision and maximizing the impact of our efforts. This realization is itself humbling—we need each other to make real and lasting change—and it illuminates how interfaith cooperation is not only a possible expression of secular humanist ethics but a requirement. If we truly "long for and strive toward a world of mutual care and concern," we must actively engage with people who are different from us.

When I was serving as an assistant chaplain at Johns Hopkins University, I organized a spring break trip for ten undergraduate students to Philadelphia focusing on interfaith encounters and social justice, with a particular emphasis on homelessness and hunger. Over the course of the week, we met with and worked alongside several excellent service organizations, including Project HOME,[4] MANNA,[5] and the Share Food Program.[6] Through the Interfaith Center of Greater Philadelphia, we coordinated visits with several different religious communities around the city to

---

4. Project HOME works to end the cycle of homelessness and poverty by providing housing, education, and healthcare in Philadelphia. For more information, visit http://www.projecthome.org.

5. MANNA, a non-profit organization in Philadelphia, provides nutritious meals to individuals battling life-threatening illnesses. For more information, visit http://mannapa.org.

6. The Share Food Program works alongside a Mid-Atlantic regional network of community organizations committed to food distribution, education, and advocacy. For more information, visit http://sharefoodprogram.org.

share in worship experiences and learn how one's experience working for social change and her religious or ethical tradition inform, inspire, and complicate each another. It was an unforgettable week, and in our short time we were able only to scratch the surface of this rich and complex subject.

Over the course of the trip, the issues of hospitality, responsibility, and humility came up time and time again. One afternoon, students met with a man who had lived on the streets of Philadelphia for twenty-five years and was now living in his own apartment and maintaining a regular job with support from Project HOME. The youngest of thirteen children, he was kept out of school, and he left home before he was fifteen. He had never learned how to read or write, which made finding work difficult. For years he felt intense anger at the ways in which people would offer assistance only on "days of service" or as a means of bolstering their own sense of self-worth. He told us how he would reject the food offered to him at Christmastime every year by "do-gooders" who would come through his cardboard village. "I am out here every day," he would tell them. "Why do you care only on Christmas that I am hungry?"

Students came away from this conversation visibly affected by his words and spent a long time discussing the importance of integrating service into our daily lives, working for systemic change so that fewer people are dependent on such service, and listening to the people we seek to assist. It was heartening that, after the trip, several students worked to design and implement a program to support people experiencing homelessness and hunger in Baltimore.

As empowering as the vision presented by the students is, it is also painfully difficult to achieve; being committed to it means that we continue to struggle to create change, knowing we will fall short. I feel great hope and gratitude in situations like the one described above, when I can help fashion "sacred spaces" in which young people from diverse backgrounds wrestle with key questions of freedom and justice, bringing their experiences and insights as Jews, Muslims, Hindus, or secular humanists to bear. In such moments, I am strengthened by the presence of a "mighty woman with a torch" calling us to light our lamps for peace and justice.

QUESTIONS FOR REFLECTION/DISCUSSION

1. What do you think Lazarus means when she writes, "Keep, ancient lands, your storied pomp!" How does this relate to her famous statement in the next sentence, "Give me your tired, your poor, your huddled masses"?

2. How do the images of the Statue of Liberty as the "Mother of Exiles" and "Lady Liberty" intersect and connect to the discussion above about peace and justice?

3. What is one key teaching for you on the virtues of hospitality, communal responsibility, or humility?

FOR FURTHER READING

Paul Rogat Loeb, ed. *The Impossible Will Take a Little While: A Citizen's Guide to Hope in a Time of Fear*. New York: Basic Books, 2004.

Jennifer Howe Peace, Or. N Rose, and Gregory Mobley, eds. *My Neighbor's Faith: Stories of Interreligious Engagement, Growth, and Transformation*. Maryknoll, NY: Orbis Books, 2012.

Esther Schor. *Emma Lazarus*. New York: Random House, 2006.

III

Sacred Practices and Interreligious Commitments

11

Meeting in the Realm of Poetry and Music

Qawwali *Devotional Music*

HOMAYRA ZIAD

The poems I share belong to the repertoire of *qawwali*, a tradition of devotional music from the multicultural and multiethnic
space of South Asian Islam. *Qawwali* is one of the most popular
musical and cultural traditions in South Asia, a region that is
home to a quarter of the world's Muslims, with multiple diaspora communities around the world, including the United States.
The word *qawwali* was adapted from the Arabic term *qawwal*
(itinerant singer, musician, storyteller) to name a new musical
genre, created by Muslims but patronized by many in South Asia
from the fourteenth century onward. Amir Khusrau of Delhi is
credited with creating this genre through the integration of Arabic, Indian, Persian, and Turkish musical traditions. Employing
well-known Indic classical and folk instruments and melodies,
qawwali began as an aid to traditional ritual meditation in the
Chishti spiritual tradition of Islam and very soon became a popular form of both devotional engagement and entertainment
among many religious groups. Islamic spirituality gave rise to
multiple vernacular literary traditions in South Asia, and
qawwali drew from a treasure trove of religious poetry, some in
classical Arabic and Persian, but much of it in local and regional
languages of the subcontinent. The poetry sung in *qawwali*

reflects local literary tropes and often uses the imagery of popular Bhakti devotionalism.[1] It draws together various Islamic devotional genres, which include praise poems for God, the Prophet Muhammad, the Prophet's family including the caliph and first imam Ali, and revered teachers of Islamic spirituality. *Qawwali* performances may take place in closed intimate circles of devotees but are also held as public events. This art form has served as a vital space for spiritual exploration and social protest, and the poetry offers searching commentary on dogmatic constructions of authority.[2]

The texts I offer below are often sung in performance contexts. Abdul Wahab Faruqi (d. 1829), also known as Sachal Sarmast ("the Truthful Ecstatic"), lived in the city of Khairpur in the province of Sindh in present-day Pakistan and wrote popular and philosophical verse in seven languages. Siraj Aurangabadi (d. 1739) lived in Aurangabad in the Deccan in present-day India. His poetry, in the forms of *masnavi* and *ghazal*,[3] has been collected in two major works and his lyrical style had a strong impact on the development of the *ghazal*.

How you've spun me 'round, darling!
—by Sachal Sarmast

How you've spun me 'round, darling!
How you've spun me 'round!

---

1. Syed Akbar Hyder and Carla Petievich, "Qawwali Songs of Praise," *Islam in South Asia in Practice*, ed. Barbara Metcalf (Princeton, NJ: Princeton University Press, 2009), 93–100.

2. Qamar al-Huda, Introduction, "Qawwali: Poetry, Performance and Politics," special issue, *Muslim World* 97, no. 4 (October 2007): 543–47.

3. *Masnavi* is a rhyming couplet. *Ghazal* is a poetic form that consists of rhyming couplets and a refrain, where each line has the same meter.

My beloved appears in human form
Oh how you've spun me 'round, darling!
You distill, you're the tavern,
you're the serving-boy.
You're the drinker, you buy the rounds
and you're the stumbling drunk, darling!

You romp around in your own lap
just like little Krishna, darling!
You sow the seeds, you tend the crops
and you're the rounding watchman, darling!

Cain and Abel were born from Adam
Who was Adam born from, darling?
You throw your Friend [Abraham] into the fire
and then you raise a ruckus, darling!

O HEAR THIS TALE OF THE WONDER OF LOVE
—by Siraj Aurangabadi

O hear this tale of the wonder of love—
where madness dissolves, the fairy has fled.
There is no more of you, there is no more of I.
There is only a certain not-knowing.

A rising wind from the unseen realm
set the garden of delight aflame.
But one small branch of sorrow's tree
—shall we call it the heart?—lived on, still green.

What a strange and wondrous time that was
when we were taught from the book of love.
The book of reason, cast aside,
left sitting on its shelf.
Siraj's heart, a beggar's bowl

was turned to ash by the fire of love.
There are no more thoughts, there is no more fear—
there is only a certain not-knowing.[4]

Interreligious encounters call for compassion, curiosity and willingness to self-critique. They demand a disciplined yet sympa-
thetic engagement with difference and the recognition that
impermeable boundaries have much to teach us about thoughtful
and generous relationship-building. The crafting of interreligious
relationships across difference calls for individual and communal
effort and the discovery of resources in our traditions that may
inspire and sustain us. In content and performance, *qawwali*
offers many lessons for interreligious relationship-building. At
the heart of this Indic musical genre lies an Islamic spiritual
impulse, and *qawwali* was often employed to popularize Islamic
devotion among new audiences. But the artists and audiences
brought to the art many devotional affiliations, as well as multiple belongings. The presence of music and the inclusive theologies of Islamic spirituality created the imaginative space for
diverse traditions to co-create and flourish.

In Islamic spirituality, music is integral to the human search
for transcendence. The Qur'an evokes a time-before-time when
God asked each unborn soul: "Am I not your Lord?" Each soul
witnessed to this reality with one voice, "Yes, indeed you are."
Our innate love of music is founded on each human being's dis-
tant memory of the beautiful voice of God on the day of this pri-
mordial covenant (*mithaq*).[5] Music recalls the joy of that moment.

---

4. Adapted from my own translations in *Kabir in Pakistan: Qawwalis and Sufi Folk Songs by Farid Ayaz and Shafi Faqir*, 2 audio CDs (Bangalore: Shrishti School of Art, Design and Technology, 2008).

5. Carl Ernst, *Teachings of Sufism* (Boulder, CO: Shambhala, 1999), 96.

It is said that on the day of the covenant, God placed a secret into the human heart. The secret is concealed like a spark in stone but blazes forth when struck with music. It is unsurprising then that Islamic civilizations offer a rich tradition of music as an aid to devotional practice. Music is present in the melodious use of the human voice as it calls to prayer (*adhan*), in the many traditions of recitation of the Qur'an, and in the practice of *dhikr*, the remembrance and invocation of God's Names, prayers for the Prophet Muhammad, and devotional poetry. Islamic spiritual traditions developed and enriched musical genres around the world. In South Asia, for example, Sufi musicians were central to the development of classical instruments like the tabla and sitar. The musical genre of *qawwali*, connected to the Chishti spiritual tradition, has engaged audiences for centuries.

Qawwali draws from the rich poetry of Islamic spirituality, which brings into high relief a fundamental Qur'anic theme: true humility arises from the knowledge that there is always more to learn. This is best expressed in the Qur'anic reminder: *wa fawqa kulli dhi 'ilmin 'alim* (Above every knower is one who knows more) and indeed in the quintessentially Islamic declaration *Allahu Akbar* (God is greater). There is a prophetic saying beloved in Muslim spiritual circles: "O God, increase my bewilderment in Thee!" These teachings remind us that the cognitive impasse of wonder at the edge of bewilderment offers a critical opening to greater self-knowledge. In spiritual poetry, bewilderment is evoked through literary devices that create cognitive dissonance, like contradiction, paradox, and imagery that shocks and unsettles.

In the first poem, Sachal Sarmast evokes a God-awareness that is grounded in wonder. He senses divine presence in every created thing and approaches each relationship with the profound humility that this entails. Yet we get the sense that the poet is also teasing us. In buoyant language, he offers up a delightful dissonance—the deity Krishna plays in his own lap, the serving boy becomes the drunk—that concurrently speaks to the unity of God. In the seamless integration of figures from theologically distinct traditions (Krishna and the biblical/Qur'anic figures Cain, Abel, and Abraham) he questions exclusivist constructions of religious identity and speaks to the reality of multiple belonging in the communities he writes for. He asks us to consider the absurdity of being held accountable for our actions by an omniscient, omnipotent God ("You throw your Friend [Abraham] into the fire and then you raise a ruckus, darling!"), a sly dig at religion that is unquestioning and dogmatic. In the simple phrase, "How you've spun me 'round, darling!" he takes joy in the knowledge that God keeps us on our toes, ever alert. It is in our embrace of wonder that we are attentive to the most profound questions of meaning.

In the second poem, Siraj Aurangabadi explores the interplay of passion (*'ishq*) and wonder, an immersive sensorial experience where the signifiers "I" and "You" no longer hold meaning. His language flirts with ambiguity, where the "you" can simultaneously signify a human beloved and God as Beloved. The ambiguity is deliberate: in Islamic spirituality, each human being is a microcosm of the divine. As we grow in conscious relationship to self and to others, we grow ever closer to God.[6] Sufi theology describes this journey of knowledge in the language of "disappearance" and "rest" (*fana* and *baqa*). When I stand before another in a conscious posture of wonder, I am open to being

---

6. In *Alchemy of Happiness*, a guide to character formation, the pre-eminent medieval scholar and systematic theologian al-Ghazzali tells us: "Know that the key to the knowledge of God, may He be honored and glorified, is knowledge of one's own self. For thus it has been said: He who knows himself knows his Lord. And it is for this that the Creator Most High said: '*We shall show them the signs on the horizons and within themselves so that it will become evident to them that it is the Truth*' (Q. 41:53)," al-Ghazzali, *Alchemy of Happiness*, lix.

fundamentally changed. There is a period of intoxication when the very presence of this person, the sheer newness, opens up possibilities of being that I may never have imagined. I stretch and expand to make room for these possibilities. I find myself flirting with ideas that may have been anathema; I reconsider my future, redraw my maps. Over time, the relationship evolves and matures—"disappearing in" becomes "resting with" (*baqa*). After ascent, descent. After intoxication, sobriety. Ultimately, I do not wish to encompass or be encompassed by my friend and conversation partner, but rather I wish to be present to her, and she to me, in the full light of day. I check back in with myself, integrate what I have learned into my systems of meaning, recalibrate and readjust. And then I thank God for letting me experience, once again, the vastness of God's creation. *Allahu Akbar*—I am humbled by what I do not know.

Aurangabadi reminds us that wonder is not a "reasonable" posture; indeed, the Book of Reason argues that it is safer for me to remain in my well-appointed comfort zone. However, Aurangabadi's poem is only echoing a Qur'anic call: *We created you all from a single man and a single woman and made you into nations and tribes so that you might come to know one another (al Hujurat, 49:13).* Our shared origin obligates us to create the conditions of encounter. In fact, the word "know" does not connote, as it could have done, mere tolerance or even a studied appreciation; rather, it is a sustained, profound, and transformative engagement. Aurangabadi's language also touches on another reality: the melancholy that is present in true encounter. He evokes a time long gone, a wonder tinged with sorrow, and a heart turned to ash in the fire of love. When we allow another human being to change us, we are enriched, but something is also lost. We must mourn who we once were even while we celebrate who we have become.

The music and poetry of *qawwali* created the imaginative space for diverse traditions to co-create and flourish. In fact, even the performance of this genre provides a template for vibrant inter-religious engagement. *Qawwali* is a dynamic, dialogical performance. Texts are hardly ever performed as whole pieces but rather as fragments of works by different poets. Fragments can entail a commingling of texts or an evocation of a text through a few words or a line. Many of these performed texts exist in several textual variants. *Qawwali* makes use of at least six different languages (Urdu, Hindi, Sindhi, Punjabi, Arabic, and Persian), and each language carries a different emotional register for the audience: "... didactic purposes are served by lines in Persian and/or Arabic, while those in vernaculars encourage emotional, experiential contemplation of the Divine."[7] Language switching is common as emotions ebb and flow. The audience and the performer are in dialogue, and the text fragments that they choose to recite or repeat depend on the reactions and expectations of the audience. *Qawwali* characterizes interreligious engagement at its best: polyphonic and supple, improvisational yet disciplined, intellectually profound yet emotionally responsive, pedagogically driven, and fundamentally open-minded.

QUESTIONS FOR REFLECTION/DISCUSSION

1. *Qawwali* has served as an important space for spiritual exploration and social protest. Are there spaces in your tradition that bring these elements or similar ones together?

---

7. Hyder and Petievich, "Qawwali Songs of Praise," 96.

2. How can writings that contain contradiction, paradox, and/or imagery that surprises or shocks help us grow spiritually?

3. What is the place of music in your religious life?

FOR FURTHER READING

Carl Earnst. *Teachings of Sufism*. Boulder, CO: Shambhala, 1999.

Kabir in Pakistan: Qawwalis and Sufi Folk Songs by Farid Ayaz and Shafi Faqir, 2 audio CDs. Bangalore: Shrishti School of Art, Design and Technology, 2008.

Barbara Metcalf, ed. *Islam in South Asia in Practice*. Princeton, NJ: Princeton University Press, 2009.

The Muslim World 97, no. 4 (October 2007) Special Issue (Qawwali: Poetry, Performance, and Politics).

Regula Qureshi. *Sufi Music of India and Pakistan*. Cambridge: Cambridge University Press, 1987.

See also the materials listed at the end of Varun Soni's essay in this volume, 120.

12

"On the Rosary of My Breath"

Nusrat Fateh Ali Khan's Mystical Fusion

VARUN SONI

On the rosary of my breath, I recite my Beloved's
name.
I know what's in my heart but only Rama knows what's
in my lover's heart.
This is my bondage, this is my prayer.
Someone's lover is in the temple, someone's lover is in
the mosque,
And I, on the rosary of my breath, recite my Beloved's
name.
I drown in the colors of love and become one with my
Beloved.
On the rosary of my love, I become Krishna.
I can't do anything else but remain intoxicated by my
Beloved's name.
With each breath, on the rosary of my breath, I recite
my Beloved's name.
My Beloved is perfect, without any fault,
While I am notorious for talking to myself!
On the rosary of my breath, I recite my Beloved's
name . . .

—Traditional Sufi poem[1]

---

1. Translated from Urdu by Varun Soni.

After I graduated from college, I spent more than a year traveling in India studying Hinduism and Islam. As part of this journey, I spent many months living in Varanasi, one of the oldest living cities in the world, or as Mark Twain famously described it, "older than history, older than tradition, older even than legend, and looks twice as old as all of them put together." Although Varanasi is known as the city of Shiva and is considered to be one of the most important Hindu pilgrimage sites in the world, it also has significant Muslim, Sikh, and Buddhist communities, histories, and houses of worship. In so many ways, Varanasi is an extraordinary interfaith city and a unique location to explore shared sacred space, song, and worship.

Living in Varanasi afforded me the opportunity to meet all sorts of interesting people representing South Asia's rich and diverse religious landscape, and as part of our weekly ritual, a core group of us would go to see the latest Bollywood musical in the movie theaters each week. The "super-hit" movie of the season was *Koyla* starring Bollywood superstars Shah Rukh Khan and Madhuri Dixit and featuring the hypnotic song "Sanso Ki Maala." But what stood out for me during the musical sequence was not Madhuri Dixit's sublime dance moves or Shah Rukh Khan's aggressive drumming, but rather the profundity of the lyrics that reflected a depth of spiritual devotion unusual for a Bollywood song. Fascinated by the melody and the lyrics, I embarked upon a search for the song's origins. I quickly learned that "Sanso Ki Maala" was originally a Sufi composition, and like many popular Bollywood songs, it had been shamelessly stolen from the canon of the late, great Nusrat Fateh Ali Khan.

Nusrat Fateh Ali Khan was the most prominent Sufi of the twentieth century and is the most famous Pakistani musician to date. He introduced millions of people around the world to the Sufi music tradition of *qawwali* while preaching a mystical message of introspection and reconciliation. One of the most popular recording artists to emerge from the South Asian subcontinent, Khan's musical virtuosity brought *qawwali* music from Pakistan's shrines to Bollywood's films and inspired a new generation of fusion musicians in the South Asian diaspora. Khan was not only the most famous ambassador of Pakistani culture, but his message of compassion and devotion embodied the highest teachings of Sufism and enabled him to unify religious and linguistic communities in Pakistan and India that had been previously divided.

Although Nusrat Fateh Ali Khan popularized *qawwali* music, its roots are more than six hundred years old. *Qawwali* is devotional music, traditionally sung by South Asian Sufi singers at religious festivals and Sufi shrines. *Qawwali* is prophetic music, propagating the music and lyrics of medieval devotional poets of South Asia. *Qawwali* is fusion music, seamlessly synthesizing instruments, rhythmic cycles, musical motifs, and poetic lyrics from diverse West, Central, and South Asian musical, literary, and religious traditions. *Qawwali* is Sufi music, invoking popular and prophetic Sufi figures as a means of inducing a mystical experience with the sublime goal being God realization. *Qawwali* is trance music, catapulting its listeners into states of rapture and intoxication, liberation and exhilaration.

As a Sufi poem, "Sanso Ki Maala," which translates into English as "On the Rosary of My Breath," incorporates the pan–South Asian poetic imagery of a lover seeking union with the Beloved: "I drown in the colors of love and have become one with my Beloved." The lover is literally going crazy waiting in vain for the Beloved to arrive: "I am notorious for talking to myself!" Ultimately the lover becomes incapacitated by love and longing: "I can't do anything else but remain intoxicated by my Beloved's name." And both Hindus and Muslims share this overwhelming devotion to the Beloved: "Someone's lover is in the temple, someone's lover is in the mosque."

"Sanso Ki Maala" is an example of the *viraha* poetic tradition, a tradition that has a long and rich history in South Asia and is oriented toward the theme of a lover longing for the Beloved, where the Beloved is a metaphor for God and the lover is experiencing the pain of separation from the divine. The most well-known example of this style stems from Hindu devotional poetry in praise of Krishna, which relates his pastimes in Vrindaban and his conjugal relationship with the *gopis* (cow maids), especially with his beloved Radha.[2] Radha feels the burden of separation when Krishna is not around, and this pain serves as a metaphor for the highest form of devotion to God. Radha's constant longing for Krishna symbolizes the individual soul's unbearable desire to be with God.

When this literary device was incorporated into the framework of South Asian Muslim devotional poetry, the poet was transformed into a feminine voice lamenting over the absence of her Beloved. The Beloved was the Prophet Muhammad, who sometimes took the guise of the bridegroom to be.[3] The poet waits for Muhammad, for the union of lover and Beloved, for only Muhammad is able to quench the intolerable thirst, cure the lovesick lover, and extinguish the agonizing flames of *viraha*.

The centrality of the *viraha* tradition is apparent when reading Jayadeva's classic *Gitagovinda*, a twelfth-century poem detailing the separation of Radha and Krishna, juxtaposed to 'Abd ur-Ra-uf Bhatti's poetry, a Muslim poet influenced by the *viraha* tradition. Notice the similarities in style and substance:

---

2. John Stratton Hawley and Mark Juergensmeyer, *Songs of the Saints of India* (New York: Oxford University Press, 1988), 99.

3. Ali Asani and Kamal Abdel-Malek, *Celebrating Muhammad: Images of the Prophet in Popular Muslim Poetry* (Columbia: University of South Carolina Press, 1995), 30.

To Krishna:

Divine physician of her heart,

The lovesick girl can only be healed with elixir from
    your body.

Free Radha from her torment, Krishna—

Or you are crueler than Indra's dread thunderbolt.[4]

To Muhammad:

Revive me so that I may live; otherwise I shall surely die

Cure me with the medicines and potions of mercy

You are the physician and the healer;

Place your hand on this weak one.[5]

The metaphor of separation plays a foundational literary role in
the evolution of the medieval South Asian Sufi poetic canon.
Such Sufi compositions are profound on a number of levels; a
mundane reading of the poetry paints a picture of a lover gone
mad with separation from the Beloved, while a more symbolic
reading illuminates the pain an individual soul feels when alien-
ated from God. Adam Nayyar, the eminent Sufi scholar and eth-
nomusicologist, highlights the literary usage of the metaphor of
separation. According to Nayyar, the analogy of separation illustrates the pain of living without the divine:

> That is a very powerful analogy that Sufi texts use. The
> fact that lovers are attracted, the fact that they join is seen
> as a divine union with the Eternal and is used as an anal-

---

4. Barbara S. Miller, *Love Song of the Dark Lord: Jayadeva's Gitagovinda* (New
York: Columbia University Press, 1977), 89.

5. Asani and Abdel-Malek, *Celebrating Muhammad*, 32.

ogy, because Sufis always try to reach you through what
you know—the pain of separation.[6]

What differentiates "Sanso Ki Maala" from other Sufi compositions, however, is that God is described in a Hindu Vaishnava
form, first as Rama and then as Krishna: "Only Rama knows
what's in my lover's heart...I become Krishna." Within some
orthodox Muslim contexts, this would be controversial, as "Sanso
Ki Maala" is a Muslim devotional song praising Hindu deities.
But within the mystical context of Sufism, "Sanso Ki Maala" is
an authentic articulation of Sufi theology.

Mysticism seeks to unite and not divide, it seeks to include,
not exclude, and for these reasons, mystics often incorporate the
language, literature, and liturgy of other mystical, devotional,
poetic, and musical traditions. So, when Nusrat Fateh Ali Khan
performed "Sanso Ki Maala" and invoked the names of popular
Hindu deities, he promoted a pan–South Asian devotionalism that
transcended the usual boundaries of religious and national identity. By drawing from the diversity of devotional and poetic traditions of South Asia, Khan brought together religious and regional
communities torn apart by sectarianism and communalism.

One such powerful moment in musical diplomacy occurred in
August 1997, when India and Pakistan celebrated their fiftieth
anniversaries of independence as nation-states. In order to com-
memorate this occasion, the Indian composer A. R. Rahman
recorded a musical piece with Nusrat Fateh Ali Khan. Together, the
most famous musician from India and the most famous musician
from Pakistan had composed "Gurus of Peace," an impassioned

6. Adam Nayyar, "Intoxicated Spirit: Nusrat Fateh Ali Khan and the Art of *Qawwali*"
(transcribed and edited by Varun Soni), *SUFI Magazine* 44 (Winter 1999): 8–12.

plea for peace between India and Pakistan. "Gurus of Peace" proved prescient, as the following year both India and Pakistan tested nuclear weapons, prompting President Clinton to call the India-Pakistan border the world's most dangerous region. But A. R. Rahman and Nusrat Fateh Ali Khan had reminded the region the year earlier that India and Pakistan could unite through musical fusion rather than divide over nuclear fusion.

Nusrat Fateh Ali Khan's performative choices also reflected his ecumenical, interfaith, and diplomatic orientation. He was a pioneer in creating new performative contexts for *qawwali*, such as world music festivals, university halls, and amphitheaters. He was also the only Pakistani musician of note to perform at Hindu temples around the world. In his own performative choices, he embodied the interfaith spirit of "Sanso Ki Maala," and this translated into a pan-South Asian embrace of Khan as both a man and a musician. Just as his lyrics brought together Hindu devotionalism and Sufi poetry, his music incorporated elements from Hindu *bhajan* music into Sufi *qawwali* music.

Looking back, it seems entirely appropriate that my quest to understand Hinduism and Islam brought me to Varanasi. My time there was spent attending Indian classical music concerts, which featured both Hindu and Muslim musicians, and spending time at *mushairas*, poetry gatherings with both Hindu and Muslim poets. As I explored this ancient city of many faiths, a city that continues to write the story of India's religions, I came to a deeper understanding and appreciation of the shared hopes, dreams, and aspirations of Indian Hindus and Muslims.

But it was not until I stumbled into a movie theater one humid day to see the latest Bollywood fare that I began to fully embrace the depth and profundity of India's religious syncretism and its history of a co-flourishing of faiths. It was not until I saw *Koyla*, a "super-hit" film starring a Hindu actress and a Muslim actor, that I began to truly understand the power of popular cultural diplomacy in bringing together Hindus and Muslims around the world. And it was not until I heard "Sanso Ki Maala," a Sufi composition reworked for the commercial masses, that I finally experienced the type of mystical intoxication that connects Hindu and Muslim devotional literature.

All of these interconnected experiences brought me to Nusrat Fateh Ali Khan, a man who dramatically shaped the trajectory of my life. Indeed, I was fortunate to spend time with his family. In fact, I helped produce a series of recordings featuring his brother and his nephew. I also served as a cameraperson for the feature-length documentary about his life entitled *A Voice from Heaven*. Finally, I wrote my doctoral dissertation about his life and legacy through the prism of prophecy, technology, and popular culture. But Nusrat Fateh Ali Khan's most enduring impact on me was to provide a template for thinking deeply about interfaith engagement, religious reconciliation, and public diplomacy. All these years later, I now can connect with a straight line the work that I do as a professor and chaplain to that fateful day two decades ago in Varanasi when I first heard "Sanso Ki Maala."

QUESTIONS FOR REFLECTION/DISCUSSION

1. "Sanso Ki Maala" is a traditional Sufi composition popularized by Nusrat Fateh Ali Khan and repackaged for a Bollywood audience. But all along it remained a sacred text for different communities. Who or what defines what a sacred text is?

2. Can you identify religious ideas or rituals that are important to you that were influenced by or contain elements from other traditions?

3. How might mystical teachings about unity and diversity help us live more peacefully with our similarities and differences?

4. How can artists and religious leaders serve together as interreligious diplomats?

FOR FURTHER READING

Pierre Alain-Baud. *Nusrat: The Voice of Faith*. Noida: HarperCollins India, 2015.

Judith Becker. *Deep Listeners: Music, Emotion, and Trancing*. Bloomington: Indiana University Press, 2004.

Jamal J. Elias, trans. *Death Before Dying: The Sufi Poems of Sultan Bahu*. Berkeley: University of California Press, 1998.

Carl W. Ernest. *The Shambhala Guide to Sufism*. Boston: Shambhala Publications, 1997.

Hazrat Inayat Khan. *The Mysticism of Sound and Music: The Sufi Teaching of Hazrat Inayat Khan*. Boston: Shambhala Publications, 1996.

Scott Kugle. *Sufis & Saints' Bodies: Mysticism, Corporeality, and Sacred Power in Islam*. Chapel Hill: University of North Carolina Press, 2007.

Adam Nayyar. *Qawwali*. Islamabad: Lok Virsa Research Center, 1988.

Regula Burckhardt Qureshi. *Sufi Music of India and Pakistan: Sound, Context, and Meaning in Qawwali*. Chicago: University of Chicago Press, 1995.

Annemarie Schimmel. *Mystical Dimensions of Islam*. Chapel Hill: University of North Carolina Press, 1975.

Varun Soni. *Natural Mystics: The Prophetic Lives of Bob Marley and Nusrat Fateh Ali Khan*. Los Angeles: Figueroa Press, 2014.

13

Sacred Debate:
Makhloket and Interreligious Dialogue

JOSHUA M. Z. STANTON

Some years ago, I experienced a Shabbat with three Mormon colleagues in Utah that made a lasting impression on me. It was a day
that defied my expectations in more ways than one, especially in
relation to matters of religious praxis, hospitality, and interreligious study and dialogue. As I think back on that day, it reminds
me of a brief, but evocative reflection by the contemporary Israeli
writer and peace activist David Grossman on the age-old Jewish
practice of *havruta* (peer) study and the place of disagreement
(*makhloket*) in such experiences.[1]

As on every Tuesday, I studied with my *havruta*
    [partners].
It's two friends, a man and a woman, with whom I
    study Talmud, Bible, and also Kafka and Agnon...
During our years of study together, we have developed
    a kind of private language of associations and
    memories.

---

1. I wish to thank my friend and teacher, Rabbi Or Rose, for sharing this text
with me and for helping me craft this essay. Our *havruta* relationship is a source of
blessing.

> I'm the nonreligious one of the three, but I've already
> had ten years of vibrant, exciting, and stormy dia-
> logue with these soulmates . . .
>
> —*Death as a Way of Life:*
> *Dispatches from Jerusalem*

I came to Salt Lake City to speak at an interfaith conference, and my gracious hosts ensured that I could observe Shabbat, including attending Saturday morning prayer services. Having done some research, we determined that the local Chabad[2] House was the best option in the area. So, first thing in the morning, three young Mormon men, all of whom had recently returned from missionary trips, took a soon-to-be Reform rabbi to an ultra-Orthodox house of prayer.[3]

From the moment we arrived at the Chabad House it was clear that we were different: my Mormon companions, respectfully donning *kippot* (head coverings), did their best to sit and stand at the appropriate moments in the service, but clearly did not understand the Hebrew or the flow of the service. And, while I was familiar with the traditional service, my multicolored prayer shawl (*tallit*)—quite common in liberal Jewish synagogues—set me apart from the other men, who were mostly wearing dark suits and traditional black-and-white *tallitot* (prayer shawls).

---

2. Chabad or HaBaD-Lubavitch is a large and influential religious community that was founded in White Russia in the late eighteenth century as part of the rise of Eastern European Hasidism (a popular Jewish mystical movement). There are Chabad Houses (synagogue and study spaces) in cities and towns throughout the world.

3. To learn more about the history and ideologies of the modern Jewish denominations, see Jonathan Sarna, *American Judaism: A History* (New Haven, CT: Yale University Press, 2005).

After the conclusion of the morning service, the rabbi kindly invited us to join him and the congregants for lunch and Torah study. In truth, by that point I felt ready to go back to my hotel room for some rest, but my Mormon hosts suggested that we stay and have a fuller Shabbat experience together. How could I refuse?

After reciting the traditional blessings over wine and bread and eating a hearty lunch, the rabbi delved into the week's Torah reading, utilizing different classical rabbinic commentaries and pausing for questions and conversation along the way. The rabbi went back and forth with different people in the room, with some challenging his ideas more directly than others. I experienced this learning session as typical of Jewish text sessions in many Orthodox and non-Orthodox religious settings. The rabbi engaged many people in the learning experience, while continuing to present his ideas. It felt normal for people to challenge him and one another openly. The rabbi was certainly recognized as the scholarly authority and spiritual guide, but he invited questions and respectful debate. This is reflective of a widespread Jewish sensibility that such rigorous discussion is a holy endeavor—one that allows individuals and communities to explore together the sacred teachings of the tradition faithfully and creatively.

To my Mormon hosts, however, the repeated challenges to the rabbi in the course of the lunchtime study session were jarring. It appeared that the students were questioning his authority and, by extension, the authority of Jewish tradition. Was this normal? Was this acceptable?

I explained to them that debate (*makhloket*) has been a time-honored tradition in rabbinic Judaism at least since 70 CE when the Second Temple in Jerusalem was destroyed by the Roman Empire. In the wake of this catastrophe, Torah study, including debate among the sages, emerged as a central Jewish practice. Textual interpretation and rabbinic dialectic became a crucial means through which to carry forth and reshape Jewish life. As Rabbi Arthur Green notes, "Judaism is a civilization built around a text." The Hebrew Bible (TaNaKh) became, in Green's words, the "new sacred center around which all of Judaism revolved."[4] Centuries later, many Jewish people—professionals and laity, religious and secular—continue to study with peers and teachers, engaging in what David Grossman describes as "vibrant, exciting, and stormy dialogue."

To my surprise, my remarks ignited an intense conversation among my hosts about the nature of truth, the relationship of Mormonism to other religions and cultures, and the place of debate within the Church of Jesus Christ of Latter-Day Saints. Interestingly, just as my hosts sat quietly and took in the synagogue discussion, I now sat quietly listening to them engage in an impassioned discussion about their faith until we reached my hotel. While the context, style, and pacing of these two conversations were quite different, it was fascinating to witness both on the same morning! Though I am not in regular contact with these remarkably hospitable young men, this unusual Shabbat adventure in Salt Lake City caused me to think anew about the dynamics of interreligious study and dialogue, including the place of disagreement and debate.

1. Dedication to a Practice

Like prayer or meditation, interreligious dialogue (whether text-based or not) is a sacred practice that requires commitment and diligence. In my experience, the most rewarding *havruta*

---

4. Arthur Green, "Torah: The People and the Book," in *Judaism's Ten Best Ideas* (Nashville: Jewish Lights, 2014), 57.

experiences—intra-Jewish or interreligious—are ones that unfold over time and contain layers of experience. In the rabbinic tradition, the ancient sages are often identified in pairs—Rav and Shmuel, or Hillel and Shammai—representing the thick bonds forged by these figures through study and conversation as well as by sharing in the joys and sorrows of life. Notice that Grossman ends his reflection by describing his partners as "soulmates"—such relationships obviously require cultivation and care, whether the participants are from a single tradition or from different ones. Even if the goal of one's dialogue is more professional than personal, sustained engagement with colleagues allows for more nuanced communication and thoughtful action.

2. What Kinds of Conversation, and When?

It is crucial to think carefully about what kinds of conversation one can engage in with her dialogue partners at different stages of a relationship. There tend to be two impulses among people involved in interreligious dialogue: avoidance of any and all conflict, or a rush to address difficult issues without proper preparation. It is crucial to establish trust before moving into the "stormy waters" of discussion. But any substantive conversation should include space for honest disagreement. As Diana Eck writes, "Dialogue does not mean everyone at the 'table' will agree with one another. Rather, it involves the commitment to being at the table—with one's commitments."[5] Of course, there are more and less productive ways of articulating our beliefs and values. I may find an idea proposed by someone else faulty, unconvincing, or even dangerous, but I must also remember that the person before

---

5. See Diana Eck, "What Is Pluralism?" http://pluralism.org/what-is-pluralism.

me was created in God's image (see Genesis 1:27) and is, therefore, to be treated with basic dignity.

3. Defining and Speaking for Ourselves

If we are going to engage in respectful and genuine dialogue, we
need to understand who we are sitting with and what matters to
them. The best way to do this is by listening intently to how our
dialogue partners understand themselves and their religious (or
secular) traditions. I appreciate the fact that Grossman felt comfortable self-identifying as a secular Jew in his reflection, and that
he and his religious *havruta* partners found a way to honor one
another's identities as they engaged together in serious discussion
over many years. It is also important to remember that no one person represents *all* Jews—religious or secular—Mormons, Hindus,
or Sikhs. In the give-and-take of dialogue, both the speaker and
listener must remember that while there may be common or
"mainstream" ideas and observances within a religious group,
there are always nuances, variants, dissenting opinions, excep-
tions, and anomalies. This sensibility is reflected in the practice of
recording both the majority and minority opinions of the sages in
the pages of the Talmud. Even if the law is fixed in accordance
with the Academy of Hillel, the ruling of the Academy of Shammai is included. Because who knows—might this idea be important to future generations?

4. Remember Why We Are Dialoguing

While *havruta* study and *makhloket* are hallmarks of rabbinic
Judaism and concepts that I believe are valuable for interreligious
engagement, I also have been in a number of study and dialogue
situations—intra-Jewish and interfaith—in which participants
(myself included) have lost sight of the purposes of the experience

and have led with ego—"Let me demonstrate how smart or learned I am." Or our ideological zeal has blocked any hope of genuine communication—"That question was answered definitively by _____ [fill in the blank!]." When tempted by such impulses, we need to ask ourselves *why* we are engaging in the dialogue. Do we simply want to convince others of the correctness of our ideas or the superiority of our religion? Or do we also want to learn with and from our dialogue partners? As I said above, the goal of a dialogue may or may not be to deepen a friendship or discover our "soulmates" (as in the Grossman text), but at root, interreligious dialogue requires mutuality and an openness to discovery in partnership with others. We may seek to persuade or influence in such encounters (as in all dialogical contexts), but are we listening? Why does this person think or believe what she does? What can I learn from her? Might I reconsider the matter, even temporarily?

While my Salt Lake City experience was brief and somewhat jagged in terms of the conversations I witnessed, the proximity and intensity of these two intra-religious discussions led me to think again about the dynamics of interreligious dialogue, including how to attend responsibly to our similarities and differences.

QUESTIONS FOR REFLECTION/DISCUSSION

1. Does the presence of the religious "other" change how you engage in discussion with people from your own religious tradition?

2. Does your demeanor, including your openness to other points of view, change when you are in dialogue with people from your own tradition or in dialogue with people from others?

3. Who have been some of your significant dialogue partners—people with whom you discuss significant theological, ethical, or existential matters?

FOR FURTHER READING

Catherine Cornille. *The Im-Possibility of Interreligious Dialogue.* New York: Crossroad, 2008.

Arthur Green. *Judaism's Ten Best Ideas: A Brief Guide for Seekers.* Nashville: Jewish Lights, 2014.

Jeffrey Rubenstein. *Rabbinic Stories.* Mahwah, NJ: Paulist Press, 2002.

Leonard Swidler. "The Dialogue Decalogue: Ground Rules for Interreligious, Interideological Dialogue," http://dialogue institute.org.

14

Biblical Exegesis as Interreligious Dialogue and Spiritual Practice

ANDREW R. DAVIS

Whenever I am asked to explain my interest in interreligious dialogue, especially between Jews and Christians, I often cite two documents from the Second Vatican Council—*Nostra Aetate* ("In Our Time," 1965) and *Dei Verbum* ("Word of God," 1965)—both of which are foundational to my work as a Roman Catholic professor of Hebrew Bible. *Dei Verbum* authorized Catholics to use critical methodologies in their study of scripture, and *Nostra Aetate* radically changed the way the Church talks about, and relates to, Jews and Judaism.[1] Just over fifty years old, these documents have made it possible for a professor like me to explore the historical and theological dimensions of scripture and to collaborate with Jewish colleagues engaged in similar study. Approached in this way, biblical exegesis becomes more than an academic pursuit; it is a spiritual practice and an opportunity for building interreligious relationships.

It may come as a surprise, then, that *Nostra Aetate* and *Dei Verbum* are not the texts that most inspire my work in interreligious dialogue. Yes, they authorize it, and they provide an

---

1. Here I use "radical" both in the sense of "fundamental" but also to allude to *Nostra Aetate*'s recognition that "[the Church] draws sustenance from the root (*radice*) of that well-cultivated olive tree onto which have been grafted the wild shoots, the Gentiles" (paragraph 4).

indispensable framework for interreligious study of the Bible, but for *inspiration* I look to an event that occurred a few years before the two documents were promulgated. The scene took place in Rome on November 26, 1961, and featured the first meeting of two people who would play key roles in the Second Vatican Council. The first person was Cardinal Augustin Bea (d. 1968), a German Jesuit priest whom Pope John XXIII had appointed to the newly created Secretariat (now Pontifical Council) for Promoting Christian Unity. The purpose of the secretariat was, and still is, to coordinate the Vatican's outreach to other Christians, and it was in this capacity that Cardinal Bea played a leading role in the writing of *Nostra Aetate*. The other figure was Rabbi Abraham Joshua Heschel (d. 1972), a Polish-born Jewish scholar who narrowly escaped the Nazi invasion of Poland and found refuge in the United States. At the time of this scene, he was a professor at the Jewish Theological Seminary in New York and was meeting with Cardinal Bea as part of a delegation of the American Jewish Committee (AJC). The AJC had been providing Bea with memoranda expressing Jewish views on various aspects of Catholic doctrine and liturgy.[2]

Their meeting produced no official document, but there is a text that came out of that meeting, which, every time I read it, inspires me to continue engaging in interreligious dialogue through the study of the Bible. The text is a memorandum of the meeting written by Zachariah Shuster, who was present as the AJC's European representative. This four-page report, circulated within the AJC a few days after the meeting, inspires me because it captures both the rapport and the challenges that can occur

---

2. Examples include "The Image of the Jew in Catholic Teaching" (June 22, 1961) and "Anti-Jewish Elements in Catholic Liturgy" (November 17, 1961).

when Jews and Christians study Scripture together.[3] In this brief essay, I will share some highlights from this AJC report, discuss how the meeting of Heschel and Bea can be a model for interreligious dialogue centered on scripture, and finally reflect on how the study of scripture in an interreligious setting has deepened my own spirituality as a Catholic and a biblical scholar.

Indeed, a key but underappreciated connection between Bea, the Catholic cardinal, and Heschel, the Jewish rabbi, was their shared background in biblical studies. Not only did both men pursue doctoral studies in Bible, but they did so at the same university. Both attended the University of Berlin, though their years of study didn't overlap. Bea was there before World War I, and Heschel completed his doctorate there a decade after that war. This common training in biblical studies is the point worth emphasizing in this opening scene between Bea and Heschel, because it was the basis of a common ground that later helped them speak with honesty and openness about sensitive issues in Jewish-Catholic relations. Shuster reports:

There was created an unusual rapport between Cardinal Bea and ourselves, representing the AJC, because thanks to Dr. Heschel we were really able to speak with Cardinal Bea, as it were, in the language of religion—as theologians coming to practical conclusions on the basis of a common language and understanding.[4]

---

3. I came upon this brief report while exploring materials in the Heschel archive at Duke University's Rubenstein Library. I am most grateful to the Institute for Catholic Thought and Culture at Seattle University for support of this research trip.

4. Shuster, memorandum to the AJC Foreign Affairs Department, December 1, 1961, p. 1.

At their first meeting, which they conducted in German, this common language was exemplified in the way Bea and Heschel acknowledged each other's scholarship in biblical studies. Bea, for example, mentioned his familiarity with Heschel's work, and Heschel, in turn, complimented Bea's work on the Song of Songs, which the cardinal had published in a critical Hebrew edition with a Latin translation. According to Shuster, "Cardinal Bea was obviously very pleased."

This rapport spilled over from the meeting, as Shuster reports in a letter, dated the same day as his memorandum (December 1, 1961), to Rabbi Marc Tannenbaum, the AJC's director of interreligious affairs. In the letter, he describes the following informal encounter between Heschel and one of Bea's assistants:

> Father Schmidt...stopped Dr. Heschel when we walked out of the interview with Cardinal Bea. He told him that he is now engaged in writing a book on the Old Testament, and that he had come across an obscure passage, which he would like to have elucidated by Dr. Heschel. Dr. Heschel made a few remarks and they left each other in the spirit of two people working on common ground.[5]

Although I would love to know the obscure passage they were discussing, it is enough to see from this encounter that the scholarly bond between Heschel and Bea was not unique to them but extended to others around them.

In the specific case of Heschel and Bea, their shared interest in biblical interpretation was more than a nice icebreaker. Hes-

---

5. Shuster, letter to Marc Tannenbaum, December 1, 1961, p. 3.

chel didn't just mention Bea's edition of Song of Songs but gifted him two volumes of traditional Jewish commentary (Midrash
Rabbah) with the section on Song of Songs bookmarked. Furthermore, Heschel opened his formal remarks with a specific reference from Bea's book in which the cardinal had quoted from
another traditional Jewish source, the Mishnah (*Yadayim* 3:5).
There was one word in the quotation, the Hebrew *olam*, which
Bea had translated into Latin as *mundus* ("world"), but that Heschel preferred to render in this case as "forever" (*olam* can carry
either a temporal or spatial meaning).[6] From here Heschel clev-
erly segued to speaking of the timeliness of their Jewish-Catholic
dialogue.

This minor issue may seem arcane, but such details are
important because they are what give texture to the story and
make it more than a general affirmation of the importance of
scripture for Jewish-Christian dialogue. Such affirmations are, of
course, indispensable, and it is not difficult to find excellent
examples within the writings of both Heschel and Bea. For example, Bea, who at this time was also helping draft *Dei Verbum*,[7] led
the way in *Nostra Aetate*'s affirmation of "the spiritual patrimony

---

6. Heschel's exploration of the dimensions of time and space is central to his philosophy of Judaism. See, for example, his classic work, *The Sabbath* (New York: Farrar, Straus and Giroux, 2005 edition [originally published in 1951]), in which he
argues that Judaism is primarily a religion of time:

> Judaism tries to foster the vision of life as a pilgrimage to the seventh day;
> the longing for the Sabbath all days of the week which is a form of long-
> ing for the eternal Sabbath all the days of our lives. It seeks to displace the
> coveting of things in space for coveting the things in time, teaching man to
> covet the seventh day all days of the week. (90–91)

7. During the drafting of *Dei Verbum* Cardinal Bea was appointed by John XXIII
as co-chair (with Cardinal Alfredo Ottaviani) of an ad-hoc committee charged with
revising the original schema that had failed to receive two-thirds approval.

common to Christians and Jews" and the "mutual understanding and respect which is the fruit, above all, of biblical...studies" (para. 4).[8] Likewise, Heschel declared after Vatican II that "a commitment to the Hebrew Bible as Holy Scripture" is "what unites [Jews and Christians]."[9]

These kinds of statements are invaluable touchstones for Jewish-Christian scriptural dialogue, but for me the story of Heschel and Bea's first meeting is just as significant because of the way the two men embody their public statements. In the AJC's account of that meeting, we witness an individual Jew and an individual Catholic putting into practice the kind of dialogue they promoted among other Jews and Catholics. In this way, their meeting models for us some key ingredients of a fruitful dialogue that is centered on scripture. The following three stand out most to me:

The first ingredient is *attention to detail*. I love that Heschel focused on the semantic range of a single word, and I love that he marked the pages in Midrash Rabbah that he thought would be relevant for Bea. And not only were these details part of their conversation, but they were preserved in the AJC's report of the meeting. The four-page report devotes an entire paragraph to the

---

8. This sentence was later quoted by the Pontifical Biblical Commission in their lengthy 2001 statement, *The Jewish People and Their Sacred Scriptures in the Christian Bible* (IV.B).

9. Heschel's comment was made during a discussion responding to papers on *Nostra Aetate* delivered by Thomas F. Stransky, CSP, and Marc H. Tannenbaum (see *Vatican II: An Interfaith Appraisal*, ed. J. Miller [Notre Dame, IN: University of Notre Dame Press, 1966], 373–74). In the same remarks Heschel stated that "the renewal of biblical studies encouraged by the document on Scripture [i.e., *Dei Verbum*] is to me, as a Jew, of equal importance [to *Nostra Aetate*]." Cf. also the later Jewish statement *Dabru Emet*, published in 2000 and signed by dozens of rabbis, which stresses that Jews and Christians "turn to [the same book] for religious orientation, spiritual enrichment, and communal education."

proper translation of the Hebrew *olam* and a whole other paragraph to the word "holy" in Genesis 2! Such attention to detail reminds me of the importance of engaging in the particularities of scripture, even—or maybe especially—in an interreligious setting. I am all for general statements affirming the importance of scripture for Jewish-Christian dialogue, but the biblical scholar in me is most excited to dig into the nitty-gritty of individual books, verses, and words. It is within these details that we find the richest common ground and also where we discover the most challenging fault lines.

Second, I love that the two men are *familiar with each other's traditions*. Bea's original quote from the Mishnah shows his engagement with traditional Jewish sources, and Heschel's gift of the volumes of midrash presumes that Bea would appreciate their value. As for Heschel, his reference to Bea's work in Latin shows that he is willing and able to read Catholic scholarship in its "native" language. Later the AJC memorandum reports that their conversation ranged from Talmudic references, to the *Sh'ma*, to the significance of the Maccabees within Jewish and Christian traditions. These features of their meeting remind me that within both Judaism and Catholicism scripture is part of a larger tradition and that shared reading of scripture is most fruitful when it engages the fullness of those traditions.

Third, I love that this exchange revolves around a point of *disagreement rather than agreement*. It's remarkable to me that Heschel kicked off his first conversation with Bea by challenging his translation of a Hebrew word. I am not sure that is where I would have started, and I do not think I am alone in this reticence. Indeed, there is a tendency in interreligious dialogue to focus on affinities between our traditions and to shy away from the differences. This approach is understandable in the beginning stages of conversation, but as trust builds, it is important to explore the divergences. And Bea's reaction is just as important as Heschel's correction. There is no defensiveness. On the contrary, the AJC report emphasizes that "the effect of this discussion among theologians obviously respecting each other was to create a warm and friendly atmosphere."[10] To me, this friendly difference of opinion on a minute issue of biblical translation set the tone for Bea and the AJC delegation to address larger theological issues, some that unite Jews and Catholics but others that divide them.

A last feature of this meeting, which inspires me to continue to engage in Jewish-Christian dialogue and study, is its attention to pastoral concerns. While the textual issues raised were somewhat technical, and the overarching agenda was focused on public policy issues, the participants expressed a shared commitment to the spiritual renewal of their religious communities. On both sides, there was a recognition that their work had to avoid repeating the historical wounds created by centuries of Jewish-Christian hostility. Although the Holocaust was not explicitly mentioned, its specter loomed throughout the meeting, especially when Heschel underlined the need for deeper knowledge of Judaism among Catholics, and when he emphasized that Jews want "to be known . . . and respected as Jews."

Further, there was a common sense among members of both groups that too many contemporary Jews and Christians felt a sense of religious malaise and existential alienation. An AJC representative at the meeting lamented that the better life many Jews had recently found in the United States had produced its own

---

10. Shuster, memorandum to the AJC Foreign Affairs Department, December 1, 1961, p. 3.

kind of religious crisis, and Bea stated that he had observed a similar problem among Christians in Western Europe despite its renewed economic prosperity. The overriding purpose of this meeting (and others related to *Nostra Aetate*) was to attend to the spiritual and pastoral needs of the Jewish and Christian communities through discussion of theological, textual, and historical matters.

While much has changed since this historic meeting in 1961, the need for interreligious dialogue and study remains crucial in a world still suffering from ignorance, bigotry, and violence. Engagement in such work is fundamentally rooted in hope. The study of scripture with someone from another tradition presumes that we have something to give to the conversation and something to receive from it. This impulse to relationship and reciprocity draws us out of our spiritual isolation and into communion with others who can expand our views of God's blessings in the world and the richness of the divine revelation that is sacred to Jews and Christians alike.

QUESTIONS FOR REFLECTION/DISCUSSION

1. How do you understand the relationship between Judaism and Christianity?

2. Have you participated in meaningful interreligious or cross-cultural study? What were some of the "ingredients" that made it memorable? Were there any challenges?

3. What is the role of knowledge in the story told above? What might we learn from Bea and Heschel in this regard?

FOR FURTHER READING

Roger Brooks, ed. *Unanswered Questions: Theological Views of Jewish-Catholic Relations.* Notre Dame, IN: University of Notre Dame Press, 1988; reprinted 1995.

John Connelly. *From Enemy to Brother: The Revolution in Catholic Teaching on the Jews, 1933–1965.* Cambridge, MA: Harvard University Press, 2012.

Edward K. Kaplan. *Spiritual Radical: Abraham Joshua Heschel in America, 1940–1972.* New Haven, CT: Yale University Press, 2007.

15

"And Among the People of the Book..."

Reading beyond Offense, Confirmation, or Gratification

SHERMAN A. JACKSON

Critical to functional bigotry is a toolbox of stereotypes, labels, and categories that can substitute for conscience, or even human experience, and do all our thinking, judging, and decision-making for us. These instruments allow us to reduce people to mono-dimensional adversaries whose moral agency is compromised and whose humanity is overshadowed by their promotion of interests or worldviews perceived to be a threat to our own. To be sure, there are bad groups and individuals in the world; and even those who are not inherently bad often end up on the opposite side of issues we hold to be vital. Sometimes, these conflicts can reduce us to genuine fear or arouse in us justifiable indignation. But sometimes our quiet little addiction to domination can push us to feign or exaggerate our fears so that we may invest in their unassailable powers of justification. Here is where negative stereotyping finds its most insidious effect. For while we and our flesh-and-blood adversaries invariably die and move on, the categories, labels, and stereotypes we construct to mark and engage them often live on in perpetuity.

It is in this context that I have been comforted by those Qur'anic verses that reflect a basic refusal to perpetuate negative, over-inclusive stereotypes. Given the starkness of many of the Qur'an's depictions and the non-linear, "arabesque" nature of its narrative, this feature of the Qur'an is often lost on non-Muslim readers who are unfamiliar with this textual style and who may stop reading upon encountering challenging or disturbing materials. And many Muslims, in their haste to enlist the Qur'an's support in this or that ideological or political conflict, routinely overlook this element as well. But it is there. Indeed, while the Qur'an unabashedly seeks to provide Muslims with the kinds of "emotionally potent oversimplifications" that Reinhold Niebuhr insisted were critical to sustaining humans in any serious socio-political struggle, it is equally keen on inoculating Muslims against the idolatry of absolutizing perspectives and attitudes born of temporal conflicts.

It is well known that the Prophet Muhammad and the nascent Muslim community faced life-threatening opposition from their Arabian kinsmen. This eventually forced them to leave their native Mecca and migrate to the northern city of Yathrib, later known as Medina. In Medina, the Prophet and the Muslims fell into conflict with groups among the local Arab polytheists and the city's Jewish residents, the latter of whom the Qur'an refers to as "People of the Book" (though the term also applies to Christians).

These conflicts between the Prophet and his "compatriots" were real and could not be casually pasted over. To begin with, his was a claim to ultimate truth. And even beyond its explicit theological assertions, his message bore significant political, socio-cultural, and economic implications. At the time, there was no state to maintain order, respond to all "citizens" equally, or protect the integrity of competing groups via a policy of "state neutrality"; there was no police force dedicated to securing everyone's safety, regardless of social status or ties of blood; there was no professional army charged with defending "the nation" against outside attack; and there was no social safety net beyond the fortunes of the tribal or religious affiliations upon which one depended for survival. Medina was an amalgamation of semi-autonomous groups held in check by a precarious "balance of fear," that is, of one group's aggressions being reciprocated by another's more devastating counter-aggressions. In this context, the emergence of any new affiliation, especially one organized around a claim to divine authority, was certain to be perceived as life-altering, if not life-threatening.

This is the backdrop against which the following verses from chapter III of the Qur'an, *The Family of 'Imrān*, must be read. They depict the ongoing conflict between the Prophet and his Jewish adversaries in Medina. On the one hand, they reflect just how high the stakes were for all involved. On the other hand, they model the importance of resisting the temptation to demonize to the point of allowing labels and group affiliations to dictate all of one's judgments.

A party of the People of the Book would love to lead you astray. But they lead astray none but themselves, while they know not. O People of the Book, why do you reject the signs of God while you are witnesses thereto? O People of the Book, why do you mix truth with falsehood; and why do you hide the truth, while you know well what you do? A party of the People of the Book even say, "Believe at the beginning of the day in that which is revealed to Those Who Believe, then reject it at the end of the day, perhaps they might turn back. And do not believe in anyone except those who follow your religion." Say [O Muhammad], "Verily, true guidance is the guidance of God." [They only say this] out of fear that someone else might be given the likes of what they have been given and proceed to argue with them on the basis thereof before God. Say [O Muhammad], "All bounty is in God's hand; He gives it to whomever He pleases. And God is expansive, wise. He singles out for His mercy whom He pleases, and God is possessed of great bounty." (3:70–74)

When these verses are taken at face value, it is easy to imagine how their sheer forcefulness could bring one to conclude that the Qur'an engages in blanket stereotyping of Jews, casting them as inherently averse to truth, lacking in piety and a basic sense of fairness, never acquiescing to a sustained or dignified existence for Islam. Such a reading would obviously offend Jews. And it might make it difficult for any Muslim who accepts the divine origins of the Qur'an to imagine anything but conflict, mutual distrust, and rancor as the presumptive modes of exchange with Jews.

Yet, two features, duly considered, directly challenge such a reading. First, while the verses repeatedly address the "People of the Book," as a rhetorical device, they make it clear that their focus is on "a party" of the group. Second, these verses are *immediately* followed by qualifiers that overturn the presumption that the characteristics in question attach to all Jews qua Jews and that Muslims and Jews, qua Muslims and Jews, are therefore doomed to perpetual conflict.

Among the People of the Book are those who if entrusted with an entire treasure will promptly return it to you. And among them are those whom if you entrust them with a single gold coin will not return it unless you stand over them importunately. That is because they say,

"We have no obligation towards these illiterates." They invent lies against God while they know full well. Nay, whoever fulfills his covenant and acts with God-consciousness, verily God loves the God-conscious. (3:75–76)

This restorative gesture is even more plainly executed a few pages later in the same chapter. Following a similarly caustic depiction of the confrontation between the Muslims and Jews (3:111–12), we read:

They are not all the same. Among the People of the Book is a party that stands at night, rehearsing God's signs, bowing in prostration. They believe in God and the Last Day, command what is right and forbid what is wrong, and they vie in doing good. These are among the righteous. Whatever good they do they will not be denied. And God is well aware of those who are God-conscious. (3:113–15)

Given the realities of our post-9/11 world, the Qur'an has become a much more public document than ever before. This has serious implications for interfaith relationships, inasmuch as many of those now consulting the Qur'an will be non-Muslims whose reading strategies diverge significantly from those that inform what Muslims generally take to be normative Islamic belief and practice. In this context, the Qur'an stands either to enhance or to erode our confidence in interfaith work. For, especially in a religious culture as infused by Protestant sensibilities as is America's (including specific hermeneutical strategies like

sola scriptura), it is vital that non-Muslims have some understanding of how Muslims read their own sacred texts. Otherwise,
outsiders to the tradition are likely to be unconvinced (or even
suspicious) of Muslim approaches to interreligious engagement
rooted firmly in the teachings of the Qur'an. In this light, I would
like to offer a few insights, based on my reading of the aforemen-
tioned verses, that may help forestall the widening of the credibil-
ity gap.

First, it is important, as these verses clearly teach us, to avoid
the practice of reading only as far as we are offended, confirmed,
or gratified. Again, given the non-linear nature of the Qur'anic
narrative style, this can be both tricky and frustrating. But one can
imagine the interpretive havoc wreaked by such an approach if we
consider, for example, stopping at the words, *"O You Who
Believe, do not approach prayer,"* ignoring what comes immediately after this, *"while you are in a state of inebriation"* (4:43).
This is especially important if the aim of consulting the Qur'an is
to engage Muslims on the basis of understandings they themselves recognize as normative, rather than imposing on them
meanings with which they do not identify.

Related to this point, these verses provide insight into a common form of religious or textual extremism. While extremism is
often thought of in terms of scriptural interpretations that don't
align with modern liberal ideals, the extremism to which I refer
is the *suppression* of verses that do not conform to our preconceived notions or ideological agendas—liberal or conservative.
In other words, to invoke Qur'anic verses on non-Muslim per-
fidy while ignoring those that point to non-Muslim goodness,
trustworthiness, or love is to go to the extreme of subordinating
scripture to the dictates of one's personal or group biases. This
applies to both Muslims and non-Muslims in their respective

attempts to deploy the Qur'an as proof of the veracity of their perspectives.

Third, these verses also point us in the direction of recognizing the difference between a divinely authored description of an *historical moment* and a divinely authored characterization of an *essential human trait*. Muslims and non-Muslims alike often read Qur'anic descriptions of Jews (or pagans or Christians) behaving in a particular manner in seventh-century Arabia as placing a religious duty upon Muslims to believe this to be the inalterable nature of every Jew until the end of time. But the Qur'anic description of Jews as "hiding the truth" is no more divinely authored than the description of them as being "among the righteous." In sum, the Qur'an does not empower one to use the *label* "Jew" to override Muslims' actual *experience* with Jews. At the same time, however, the fact that Jews in twenty-first-century America may act very differently from the behavior ascribed to a particular group of seventh-century Jews in Medina does not disprove the historicity of the Qur'anic account. Both of these insights are critical to the health, integrity, and transparency of interfaith relations. For, on the one hand, Jews and Christians can hardly be expected to maintain confidence in interfaith work if they believe that Muslims are Qur'anically bound to see them as perfidious. At the same time, traditional Muslims will not negate the historical claims of the Qur'an simply to avoid offending contemporary Jews, Christians, or others who view descriptions of ancient historical events as timeless and essential descriptions of their communities.

Fourth, these verses make no attempt to deny the tragic reality of human conflict. As people of faith, we must be prepared to acknowledge that our values and principles, if we are truly committed to them, may bring us into conflict with others. For to avoid *all* conflict is to dismantle the boundaries between Judaism, Christianity, and Islam. The aim as such must be to *avoid* all the conflicts that we can avoid and to *manage* the conflicts we cannot avoid with courage, humility, and God-consciousness. Moreover, we must avoid the tendency (to which religious groups seem distinctly prone) to raise every conflict beyond the terrestrial plane into the realm of the transcendent, where conflicts morph into epic battles between absolute good (us) and permanent evil (them). Not all conflicts between Jews, Christians, or Muslims are religious or reducible to good versus evil. I see nothing, for example, absolutely good or evil about supporting or opposing Obamacare *or* any of its rivals. And even where the conflict among us is religious, these verses remind us that this should not be taken as a justification for the self-serving suspension of morality: it should have no bearing, for example as we see in the verses, on whether we return each other's entrusted wealth.

Finally, whether the point of contention is religious or nonreligious, we should be careful not to infuse our labels and categories with so much weight and power that they ultimately turn against us by denying us the ability to get beyond our own inventions. When members of our communities infuse terms like "Jew," "Muslim," and "Christian" with transcendent, congenital dread, they pass on to their descendants viruses that totally degrade their faculties for human encounter. Saturated with such dread, the categories we bequeath to our heirs threaten to overpower their ability to interface on a basic human level.

Let us be reminded by these verses and pass on to posterity: "*They are not all the same.*" And let us remember, as the Qur'an also tells us: "*Good deeds and evil deeds are not equal. Repel [evil deeds] with deeds that are better; you will find that he between whom and you there was enmity [will become] as if he were a longstanding trusted friend*" (41:34). And God knows best.

QUESTIONS FOR REFLECTION/DISCUSSION

1. How do we reconcile scriptural descriptions of religious others with our actual experience of those others?

2. How can we prevent scripture from being a barrier rather than a help to interfaith cooperation?

3. How do you understand the historical claims made in the TaNaKh, New Testament, the Qur'an, or other canonical texts?

FOR FURTHER READING

Sherman A. Jackson. "Jihad and the Modern World." *Journal of Islamic Law and Culture* 1 (2002): 1–26.

Ingrid Mattson. *The Story of the Qur'an: Its History and Place.* Edinburgh: Wiley-Blackwell, 2013.

Mustansir Mir. *Understanding the Islamic Scripture.* New York: Routledge, 2007.

Fazlur Rahman. *Major Themes of the Qur'an.* Chicago: University of Chicago Press, 2009.

16

Unity and Multiplicity

The Practice of Sohila and Sikh Theology

SIMRAN JEET SINGH

Sikhs recite *Sohila* in the evening as part of their daily discipline. This work comprises five compositions (*shabads*) written by three Gurus. The first three *shabads* were composed by the founder of the tradition, Guru Nanak (d. 1539 CE), and the last two were written by Guru Ramdas (d. 1581) and Guru Arjan (d. 1606). *Sohila* appears on pages 12 and 13 of the Guru Granth Sahib, the Sikh scripture, in the section that is often referred to as *Nitnem* (literally "Daily Practice").

According to early sources, Sikhs have been singing *Sohila* from the time of Guru Nanak and his community in Kartarpur. Reciting and singing this *bani* (scriptural work) offers one the opportunity to reflect on the day and look forward to the future with urgency and optimism. The central message of *Sohila* is to live in constant remembrance of the Divine while seeking to make the most of one's life. Below, I explore excerpts from each of the five sections of this prayer that are particularly important to Sikhs involved in interfaith initiatives.

In the Rag of Dipaki, by Guru Nanak

One Universal Creator.
By the True Guru's grace.
The house in which praises are expressed
and the Creator is contemplated,
in that house, sing the song of joy and remember the
Maker...

Shabad 1—Whom Do We Admire?

The first *shabad* opens with a focus on identifying who it is that we ought to admire in this world. The opening lines of this *shabad* set the stage for interreligious engagement by demonstrating that one is not to be admired for his or her religious affiliation or other outward markers. Guru Nanak does not say that we should praise those who have decided to accept the Sikh way of life. Rather, he states that we ought to associate with those who have cultivated a relationship with the Divine, the "Universal Creator."

This reflects the pluralistic outlook of Sikhism. The Gurus did not believe that one must embrace the Sikh tradition in order to forge a relationship with the Divine. What is more important from their perspective is that one is engaged in spiritual development that is rooted in love and remembrance of the Divine.

This outlook is evident in the lives of the Sikh Gurus as well. One can see it in the friendships they forged with spiritual leaders from other religious traditions and in their decision to include writings from voices outside of their community in the Sikh canon.

IN THE RAG OF ASA, BY GURU NANAK

There are six philosophical schools, six teachers,
and six teachings.[1]
. . .
There are countless seconds, minutes, hours, days,
    weeks, and months—
There is one sun, yet [there are] many seasons—
O Nanak, the Creator has numerous forms!

Shabad 2—Oneness and Plurality
The recognition of difference is fundamental to our human experience, and it poses a challenge to understanding that the world is, in fact, one integrated whole. Guru Nanak addresses this challenge in his second *shabad* by offering practical examples of how we might view plurality within unity.

Perhaps the most instructive moment in this composition comes when Guru Nanak discusses how we have come to understand time. He writes that there are divisions that humans have created in order to organize and inhabit time, from milliseconds and minutes to months and years. He recognizes the utility of these increments and therefore does not reject these as unhelpful or unreal—and then he delivers the punch line: each of these increments is mediated by a single source, the sun. Such is the way of the world.

---

1. This phrase refers to traditional Hindu approaches that posit six philosophical systems (Mimamsa, Nyaya, Vaiseshika, Sankhya, Yoga, and Vedanta), each of which has a distinct text (*shastra*), a distinct author (*guru*), and a distinct teaching or worldview (*updes*).

Guru Nanak's ability to reconcile the diversity of our world with a vision of Divine oneness figures centrally in my approach to interreligious engagement. From a Sikh perspective, difference is not a problem that has to be solved, nor is difference a threat that must be eliminated. For Sikhs, difference is something we celebrate, as the diversity of this world serves to remind us of the magnificence and vastness of the Divine. I believe deeply that we must bring an appreciation for our similarities and differences to the interreligious table. We must acknowledge what binds us together while also acknowledging and appreciating what makes us different.

IN THE RAG OF DHANASARI, BY GURU NANAK

... You have thousands of eyes, yet no eyes.
You have thousands of forms, yet no single form.
You have thousands of feet, yet no feet.
You have no nose, yet thousands of noses.
I am enchanted by Your wonders!
The Divine light is within all. That light is the One.
The light of the One is the light within all ...

Shabad 3—The Light of the Divine Is the Light within All
Guru Nanak sees the divine form all around him, yet he states that the Divine has no particular form. He then explains this paradox by picking up a thread from the previous *shabad*: the light of the Divine is the same light within all, and this divine light infuses all of creation. Every aspect of life is equally imbued with divine light, and therefore everything and everyone is holy. Recognizing

all to be inherently divine is fundamental to Sikh theology and has direct bearing on Sikh principles of equality, justice, and service. No aspect of Sikh theology allows for discrimination, whether on the basis of one's gender, socioeconomic status, or religious conviction. The idea that each and every person is infused with the same divine light leads to a strong emphasis in Sikhism on service and social justice efforts, both within and beyond the Sikh community.

In the Rag of Gauri Purbi, by Guru Ramdas

The village is overflowing with desire and anger.
These vices are conquered in meeting the Guru.
With fortune recorded, I have met the Guru
and have been immersed in Divine love...

Shabad 4—Removing the Thorn of Ego

The fourth *shabad* of *Sohila* is composed by the fourth Guru of the Sikh tradition, Guru Ramdas (d. 1581 CE). This *shabad* views the human experience through a critical lens and focuses on various distractions in life, such as anger and lust, that keep us from reaching our ultimate objectives. Guru Ramdas points to ego as the primary source of unhappiness in our lives. Later in this same passage he compares it to a "thorn in the foot." So long as we try to walk without removing the thorn of ego, it will continue to cause us and others pain.

According to Guru Ramdas, the solution for the problem of ego is to cultivate humility. Putting one's self in the company of more accomplished people, showing deference to those who have achieved that to which we aspire, and acting thoughtfully for others are ways to limit our self-centeredness. Humility and respect are foundational principles that inform how Sikhs have come to approach interreligious engagement. Every interaction is an opportunity to learn, to share, to serve, and to help remove the thorn of ego.

In the Rag of Gauri Purbi, by Guru Arjan

Listen my friends, I make this request:
now is the time to serve the devotees!
Earn divine profit now and live with joy in the future.
Time is decreasing by day and night...
O Inner-Knower, O Creative Being, please fulfill my one
   yearning.
Servant Nanak requests only this happiness:
"Make me the dust of the devotees' feet!"

Shabad 5—A Sense of Urgency
The fifth and final *shabad* of Sohila was composed by Guru Arjan (d. 1606 CE) and focuses on the urgency of life. We have but a limited time on this earth, and this human life is a unique opportunity to connect with the Divine. The recognition that our days are numbered ought to push us to focus on spiritual growth. Guru Arjan reminds us that this is not an easy journey and that we need guidance and support to accomplish our goals. The happiness that he requests at the end of the *shabad* is telling: "Make me the dust of the feet of the saints!" This final line reminds us again of the need for divine *and* human support. By putting

ourselves in the company of teachers and fellow devotees, we substantially increase the likelihood of cultivating a relationship with the Divine.

This formulation is central to my interreligious work. I am attracted to this sphere because it is filled with spiritual seekers of various faith traditions whom I admire and from whom I learn so much. We may be members of different religious communities, but I resonate deeply with their efforts in discovering God's light and shaping their lives in ways that are reflective of this ultimate goal. It is with such people that I wish to work, and it is in this wondrous world of diversity within unity that I wish to serve.

QUESTIONS FOR REFLECTION/DISCUSSION

1. How do you understand the relationship between the unity and diversity of the world?

2. What is the role of remembrance in your tradition? How is it expressed ritually?

3. The Gurus serve as sources of wisdom and as role models to Sikhs. Who are some of the figures in your religious or cultural heritage who inspire you?

FOR FURTHER READING

Max Arthur Macauliffe. *The Sikh Religion: Its Gurus, Sacred Writings, and Authors*. Oxford: Oxford University Press, 1909.
Eleanor Nesbitt. *Sikhism: A Very Short Introduction*. Oxford: Oxford University Press, 2016.

Harbans Singh. "Sohila." In *The Encyclopedia of Sikhism*. Patiala: Punjabi University, 1997.

Nikky Guninder Kaur Singh. *The Name of My Beloved: Verses from the Sikh Gurus*. San Francisco: Penguin, 2003.

Sahib Singh. *Guru Granth Darpan* [in Punjabi]. New Delhi: Punjabi Prakashan, 1966.

IV

Interreligious Engagement and the Public Square

17

Opening the Door

Imam Ali and New Conversations in Interreligious Dialogue

HUSSEIN RASHID

The image normally sits in a two-by-three-inch frame. It was created in Iran and given to me as a gift. It is a popular image, and the artist's name is unknown. As a mass-produced illustration, it can be found found in a variety of sizes and is usually hung on walls or placed on tables.

This image is of Ali ibn Abi Talib, or Imam Ali, considered by many Muslims to be the inheritor of the Prophet Muhammad's religious knowledge. Many Sufi orders trace their spiritual teaching back to him. This particular image is popular in Shi'ah communities, those who believe that Imam Ali was the rightfully designated successor to the Prophet Muhammad, and that the children of Imam Ali and Bibi Fatima, the Prophet

Muhammad's daughter, possess the *nur* (light) of guidance. This light is passed from generation to generation, through Divine appointment. Our discussion of this image will draw on Shi'ah theology, but the ideals the image represents are common across Muslim communities.

The use of an image allows believers to regard Imam Ali as a means for the remembrance of God and to contemplate the example that Imam Ali sets for his *murids* (followers). As an artifact, the image enmeshes the viewer within cultural complexes and historical memories. Imam Ali was known for his eloquence in speech and writing and as a source of moral guidance and a model of correct *adab* (behavior). And like the ritual of the *Hajj*, during which Muslims collapse moral time and take on the attitudes of the Prophet Ibrahim (Abraham), Bibi Hajirah (Hagar), and the Prophet Ismail (Ishmael), the image reminds the viewer to behave with the same sense of justice as did Imam Ali.[1]

The image serves as a useful point of discussion, not for introductory conversations about Muslim belief but for a more nuanced deliberation on the different ways of being Muslim. A discussion about an image of Imam Ali is a productive way to engage with groups who have some basic understanding of Muslim thought and communities of interpretation. The image opens conversation on diversity within Muslim communities and misperceptions regarding the place of art and images in lived religion. It may also move audiences to a deeper understanding of spirituality, prayer, and practice. An object like a framed picture or *tasbih* (prayer beads) also directs us to the material nature of religion: religion is not just about personal belief, but also about

---

1. M. Ali Lakhani, Reza Shah-Kazemi, and Leonard Lewisohn, eds., *The Sacred Foundations of Justice in Islam: The Teachings of ʿalī Ibn Abī Ṭālib* (Bloomington, IN: World Wisdom, 2006).

community building. Many religious traditions invest in the production of material objects—whether architecture, clothing, or dinnerware—as an expression of belief. These objects help bound and bind a community, and they define what the members of that community believe.

One of the basic groupings of Muslims is Shi'ah. The Shi'ah believe that Prophet Muhammad designated Imam Ali as his successor. This belief comes from the revealed word of God in the Qur'an and from the Prophet Muhammad's own words. One *hadith* (a saying of the Prophet) tells us that Imam Ali is to the Prophet Muhammad as the Prophet Harun (Aaron) was to the Prophet Musa (Moses), except that he, Imam Ali, would not be a prophet. Since the Prophet Harun was a clear successor to the Prophet Musa, Ali became the first Imam, or divinely appointed guide for the community.

The Qur'an says that every community, through all time and history, has a guide, and therefore, that guidance could not have ended with the death of the Prophet. In addition, the Prophet Muhammad said that he left behind two weighty things, the Qur'an and his family, and as long as people followed both, they would never be led astray. The Qur'an implicitly mentions Imam Ali (5:55, 4:59, 36:12) and his children as the heirs of the Prophet (33:33, 42:23), and explicitly tells the Prophet to declare Imam Ali's succession (5:67), ultimately saying that the religion would be perfected once the declaration had been made (5:3).

One role of the Imam is to perform some of the religious functions of the Prophet. For example, he takes *bayah*, or allegiance to God on behalf of the community (48:10) and serves as an intercessory figure. Intercession is mentioned many times in the Qur'an (39:44, 2:255, 34:23), but ultimately the argument is that God grants this power to chosen individuals (34:4, 10:4).

The Prophet Muhammad was one of those individuals (48:10, 4:64, 33:56).

Imam Ali is an exemplar of intellect, wisdom, and chivalry. His letters, teachings, and sermons are collected in *Nahj ul-Balagha, The Peak of Eloquence*, so named because of the grace and beauty with which he wrote. Speaking of the creation of our nature, he writes:

> Then [God] breathed into it [the human form of clay] of [the Divine] spirit, and it stood up as a human being, endowed with intellectual powers with which to reflect, thoughts by which to conduct himself, limbs to put to service, instruments at his disposal, and knowledge.[2]

One of Imam Ali's most famous letters as caliph was written to his governor in Egypt. In the letter Imam Ali admonishes the governor to remember to care for the citizens with the mercy with which God has treated him; his first obligation is to those who would ordinarily not have access to him, because they are the ones who are most easily forgotten.[3]

Imam Ali serves as a metonym for other Imams. Because the line of guidance is continuous and divinely ordained, we find great consistency in the teachings of the Imams across time. Imam Zayn al-Abidin (AS)[4] (d. 713), the grandson of Imam Ali, is famed for his book of prayers, *As-Sahifa As-Sajjadiyya*.[5] In this

---

2. Reza Shah-Kazemi, *Justice and Remembrance: Introducing the Spirituality of Imam Ali* (London: IB Tauris, 2006), 210.

3. Ibid., 219–34.

4. The letters "as" used after the name of a prominent religious figure among Muslims signify the words *alayhi salam*, which mean "upon him (or her) be peace."

5. ʿAlī ibn al-Ḥusayn Zayn al-ʿĀbidīn, *The Psalms of Islam: Al-Ṣaḥīfat Al-Kāmilat Al-Sajjaādiyya*, trans. William C. Chittick (London: Muhammadi Trust of Great Britain and Northern Ireland, 1988).

cycle of prayers, we are reminded of our obligations to the Divine and to our fellow humans. Imam Jafar as-Sadiq (AS) (d. 765), considered one of the most brilliant minds of Islamic law, states in his *Lantern on the Path* that human action is defined by four areas of conduct: with God, with ourselves, with each other, and with the rest of creation. He declares that not considering all of these in a complete whole is a failure of faith.[6]

The famous Persian poet, Jalaluddin Rumi (d. 1273), tells a tale of Imam Ali (AS) and his qualities of mercy. The Imam is in battle and has defeated an enemy in a duel. As he is about to deliver the deathblow, his enemy spits in his face. Imam Ali puts his sword away. When asked why, he says that when he was spat upon, he became angry and began fighting on behalf of his ego and his anger, forgetting God. This tale has become a popular reminder to remember God and stay true to one's convictions, even in the most difficult situations. Rumi's reverence for Imam Ali highlights the special status of Ali in a wide variety of Muslim communities. Among non-Shiah communities, he is often revered not as an Imam but as a *wali*, a "friend of God." These groups also recognize other *awliya*, or friends of God, and use reverential images of these figures in a manner similar to the ways in which this image is used.

For example, in Senegal, members of the Sufi group known as the Muridiyya often display images of Sheikh Amadou Bamba, the founder of the order. In the words of one Muridi, the image of Amadou Bamba:

> prevents me from going in a bad direction because the image is a protection . . . There is no limit to his blessings . . .

---

6. Jaʿfar al-Ṣādiq, *The Lantern of the Path,* trans. Fadhlalla Haeri (Dorset: Element Books, 1989).

> The image attracts good fortune and repels evil... This is
> why when the Mourides find themselves in difficult situ-
> ations, they say that they will surmount them with the
> *baraka* [spiritual presence] of the Holy Man...

> The image gives me confidence. One can just look at the
> picture and see an image, but I look to see the inside of
> the Holy Man. And the Holy Man doesn't have any bad
> side. He is good through and through. The image brings
> only happiness and good fortune. I know that I have the
> power of the Holy Man within me. This is what is allow-
> ing me to talk to you right now.[7]

For groups who do not emphasize intercession, the use of an
image presents the risk of idolatry. Nasir ud-Din Tusi, a famous
thirteenth-century Persian thinker, says that to the uninitiated a
conflation between the name and the named is common. For those
who seek and are trained in true knowledge, there would be no
confusion between the word "rose" and an actual rose. In a similar vein, the friends of God serve as reminder, pointing a believer
toward God.[8] In the Qur'an, the nature of God can be understood
as utterly transcendent, like an indescribable light (24:35), or so
immanent that God is closer to us than our own jugular vein
(50:16). By focusing on a figure like Imam Ali, Muslims find a
way to navigate between the transcendence and immanence of the
divine nature. Just as the Prophet served as someone to whom
believers could relate, who could help open their hearts to the

---

7. Allen F. Roberts, et al., *A Saint in the City: Sufi Arts of Urban Senegal* (Los
Angeles, California: UCLA Fowler Museum of Cultural History, 2003), 48.

8. Nasir al-Din Tusi, *Contemplation and Action,* trans. S. J. Badakhchani (New
York, NY: I. B. Tauris, 1995).

majesty of God, the *awliya* fulfill a similar responsibility. There-fore, to those who do accept the Qur'anic idea of the Imam, the images and reminders of the friends of God actually serve as a reminder of *tawhid* (monotheism) rather than as a temptation to idolatry.

It is this that animates me as a Shi'ah Isma'ili Muslim: to know that God is with us at all times and has left us the family of his beloved, the mercy to all creation, to continue to guide us. It is through the prophetic guidance embodied through the *ahl ul-bayt*, the family of the Prophet, that I am constantly reminded of God, and reminded to cultivate *taqwa*, God-consciousness. Whether through the guidance of the Aga Khan, the present, living Imam, or Imam Ali, I know that our task as believers remains ongoing.

Imam Ali says that faith guides us to deeds, and deeds guide us to piety.[9] Coupled with Imam Jafar's guidance that we are responsible to one another and the Qur'anic injunction to know one another (49:13), I am compelled to build community. Inter-faith dialogue through words and deeds is one component of that engagement. Ultimately, it is to create justice in the land, and Imam Ali says justice rests on four pillars: deep comprehension, abundant knowledge, blossoms of wisdom, and flowerbeds of restraint.[10] He expands on these principles when he states:

> Justice also has four aspects: keen understanding, deep knowledge, a good power of decision, and firm forbear-ance. Therefore, whoever understands comes to acquire

---

9. ibn Abī Ṭālib ʿAlī, Jāḥiẓ, and Muḥammad ibn Salāmah Quḍāʿī, *A Treasury of Virtues: Sayings, Sermons and Teachings of ʿalī with the One Hundred Proverbs Attributed to Al-Jāḥiẓ*, trans. Tahera Qutbuddin (New York: New York University Press, 2013), 135.

10. Ibid., 137.

depth of knowledge; whoever acquires depth of knowledge drinks from the spring of judgment; and whoever
exercises forbearance never commits evil actions in his
affairs and leads a praiseworthy life among the people.[11]

These pillars arise from engagement and learning with others, not through individual contemplation. We can understand
one another only by being with one another, acquiring knowledge, and cultivating empathy. Empathy brings the ability to
judge fairly. And justice involves equity; it must recognize the
rights of all people.

Where discussions regarding the image of Imam Ali become
difficult is around questions of representation. While Imam Ali is
not universally recognized as an Imam, it is a rare Muslim community that does not hold him in some sort of esteem and continue to learn from his teachings. However, there is a common
misperception that figural representation is forbidden by "Islam."
This point allows us to engage with the idea that "Islam" is not a
monolith. Rather, it is a religious tradition made up of people. It
is the people, Muslims, who speak. And here, material culture can
show us what Muslims do based on their beliefs.

While Muslim belief generally prohibits the use of images in
mosques, the image of Imam Ali demonstrates that it does not
completely prohibit the creation and use of images. There are
people and animals represented in Mughal and Persian minia-
tures. The tradition of representing the *awliya*, or friends of God,
is a long one, and exists across Sunni and Shi'ah traditions. There
are also places besides mosques where Muslims pray, and images
are not only accepted but also expected. This point drives home

---

11. Ali ibn Abu Talib, *Nahjul Balagha: Peak of Eloquence: Sermons, Letters, and Sayings of Imam Ali Ibn Abu Talib* (Elmhurst, NY: Tahrike Tarsile Quran, 1984), 576–77.

the diversity of Muslim communities, emphasizing the existence of places of worship besides the mosque, and the roles these places play for Muslims.

The contemporary "rule" against representing Muhammad is very new in terms of how it is applied across Muslim communities. It is a minority opinion that, for a variety of historical and economic reasons, is believed to have been generally agreed upon by all Muslims. Instead, the image of Imam Ali shows one of the ways in which Muslims have in fact turned to the likenesses of religious figures for guidance and moral encouragement. From here, we can begin discussing the role of politics and economics in the formation of religious ideas and in how they spread. More important, we have here a good basis for arguing against religious illiteracy, which leads to the acceptance of the loudest, most puritanical voices as the most "authentic" when it comes to any religion, as though brutality were the marker of true piety.

The image of Imam Ali serves as a way to explore Muslim spirituality more deeply. For example, he is connected to Sufism, a deeply personal and philosophical approach to the faith shared by both Shi'ah and Sunni. Even today, however, the diversity of Sufi thought remains unexplored in most interfaith gatherings. Most important, Imam Ali serves to challenge the simplistic idea that Shi'ah and Sunni have never gotten along. Muslims believe that the Angel Jibrail (Gabriel) came to Prophet Muhammad and said, "There is no hero except for Ali."[12] I believe Imam Ali continues to be a hero for today's world: as the first Shi'ah imam, and representative of the continuing nature of Imamate, Imam Ali opens up for us the vast number of ways that one can be a Muslim.

---

12. Shah-Kazemi, *Justice and Remembrance*, 15.

QUESTIONS FOR REFLECTION/DISCUSSION

1. The image of Ali helps bound a community while demonstrating layers of communal belonging. Think about an object like the Hand of Fatima (*yad/khamsa*), an artifact of a culture shared across religious communities. Are there cultural objects or references we share as Americans that bind us together as a nation?

2. What sorts of objects do you have strong feelings for? Why? How did you learn to revere these objects?

3. Sufi Comics (http://www.suficomics.com) is a website that presents the teachings of Imam Ali in an illustrated format. What are some ways in which religious traditions are engaging with contemporary art forms?

FOR FURTHER READING

'Alī ibn Abī Ṭālib, Jāḥiẓ, and Muḥammad ibn Salāmah Quḍā'ī. *A Treasury of Virtues: Sayings, Sermons and Teachings of 'Alī With the One Hundred Proverbs Attributed to Al-Jāḥiẓ*. Edited and translated by Tahera Qutbuddin. New York: New York University Press, 2013.

Ja'far al-Ṣādiq. *The Lantern of the Path*. Translated by Fadhlalla Haeri. Dorset: Element Books, 1989.

M. Ali Lakhani. Reza Shah-Kazemi, and Leonard Lewisohn, eds. *The Sacred Foundations of Justice in Islam: The Teachings of 'alī Ibn Abī Ṭālib*. Bloomington, IN: World Wisdom, 2006.

Allen F. Roberts, Mary Nooter Roberts, Gassia Armenian, and Ousmane Guáeye. *A Saint in the City: Sufi Arts of Urban*

Senegal. Los Angeles UCLA Fowler Museum of Cultural History, 2003.

Reza Shah-Kazemi. *Justice and Remembrance: Introducing the Spirituality of Imam Ali.* London: I. B. Tauris, 2006.

Reza Shah-Kazemi *Spiritual Quest: Reflections on Qur'anic Prayer According to the Teachings of Imam 'Alī.* London: I. B. Tauris, 2011.

Nasir al-Din Tusi. *Contemplation and Action.* Translated by S. J. Badakhchani. New York: I. B. Tauris, 1995.

Zayn al-ʿĀbidīn, ʿAlī ibn al-Ḥusayn. *The Psalms of Islam: Al-Ṣaḥīfat Al-Kāmilat Al-Sajjaādiyya.* Translated by William C. Chittick. London: Muhammadi Trust of Great Britain and Northern Ireland, 1988.

18

Swami Vivekananda's Address to the First Parliament of the World's Religions on September 11, 1893

Jeffery D. Long

The first Parliament of the World's Religions was held in Chicago in the autumn of 1893. This event, very much a product of its era, was an extension of the Columbian Exposition or World's Fair of 1893. An event intended to showcase human progress in a wide array of fields, from culture to technology, the Exposition and the Parliament that accompanied it, while highlighting human cultural diversity—and thus being, in many ways, a cutting-edge event for its time—nevertheless carried a definite note of Western triumphalism: that it was in the West, and America in particular, that human potential had achieved its true height of greatness. Even many of the participants in the Parliament, progressive thinkers who were spearheading the nascent interfaith movement of that time, saw the function of interreligious dialogue as "preparing the way for the reunion of all the world's religions in their true center, Jesus Christ."[1]

---

1. John Henry Barrows, *The World's Parliament of Religions: An Illustrated and Popular Story of the World's First Parliament of Religions, Held in Chicago in Connection with the Columbian Exposition of 1893* (Chicago: Parliament Publishing Company, 1893), 25. The quote in question is attributed to Bishop Charles C. Grafton of Fond du Lac.

Into this context strides Swami Vivekananda, a Hindu monk and the pre-eminent disciple of Sri Ramakrishna, a Bengali mystic who had passed away just seven years earlier. In the years since his master's passing, Vivekananda had traveled the length and breadth of India on foot as a simple *sannyasi*, or renouncer, seeking a way to spread the message of his master and to regenerate the spiritual life of the people of India, who were laboring under the crushing heel of British imperialism. Encouraged by the Raja of Ramnad, a ruler in southern India who had become his disciple, Vivekananda had resolved to travel to America and participate as a Hindu representative to the Parliament. His goal was to make the case, in the heart of the Western world, for the global relevance of Hindu thought and spirituality.

It was an act of supreme audacity. Vivekananda's courage was fueled, however, by his devotion to his master's teaching: *yato mat, tato path*: "Every religion is a path." This teaching was a way to the supreme realization attested to in the Hindu scriptures for thousands of years, that the presence of divinity inheres in all beings and that the ultimate aim of our existence is the manifestation of this divine potential.

Speaking truth to power, not unlike the biblical prophets, Vivekananda delivered this message as an Indian at a time when European colonization of much of the earth was being justified as the "white man's burden" and as a Hindu in a land where the superiority of Christianity was taken for granted. Vivekananda thus paved the way for his countryman, Mohandas K. Gandhi, who that same year was thrown off a train in South Africa for the crime of riding in a first-class compartment while Indian, an incident that would spark a nonviolent revolution.

Swami Vivekananda's Response to Welcome
at the World's Parliament of Religions, Chicago
11th September 1893

Sisters and Brothers of America,

It fills my heart with joy unspeakable to rise in response to the warm and cordial welcome which you have given us. I thank you in the name of the most ancient order of monks in the world; I thank you in the name of the mother of religions; and I thank you in the name of millions and millions of Hindu people of all classes and sects.

My thanks, also, to some of the speakers on this platform who, referring to the delegates from the Orient, have told you that these men from far-off nations may well claim the honour of bearing to different lands the idea of toleration. I am proud to belong to a religion which has taught the world both tolerance and universal acceptance. We believe not only in universal toleration, but we accept all religions as true. I am proud to belong to a nation which has sheltered the persecuted and the refugees of all religions and all nations of the earth. I am proud to tell you that we have gathered in our bosom the purest remnant of the Israelites, who came to Southern India and took refuge with us the very year in which their holy temple was shattered to pieces by Roman tyranny. I am proud to belong to the religion which has sheltered and is still fostering the remnant of the grand Zoroastrian nation. I will quote to you, brethren, a few lines from a hymn which I remember to have repeated from my earliest boyhood, which is every day repeated by millions of human beings, *"As the different streams having their sources in different places all mingle their water in the sea, so, O Lord, the different paths which men take through different tendencies, various though they appear, crooked or straight, all lead to Thee."*

The present convention, which is one of the most august assemblies ever held, is in itself a vindication, a declaration to the world of the wonderful doctrine preached in the Gita: "Whosoever comes to Me, through whatsoever form, I reach him; all men are struggling through paths which in the end lead to me." Sectarianism, bigotry, and its horrible descendant, fanaticism, have long possessed this beautiful earth. They have filled the earth with violence, drenched it often and often with human blood, destroyed civilisation and sent whole nations to despair. Had it not been for these horrible demons, human society would be far more advanced than it is now. But their time is come; and I fervently hope that the bell that tolled this morning in honour of this convention may be the death-knell of all fanaticism, of all persecutions with the sword or with the pen, and of all uncharitable feelings between persons wending their way to the same goal.[2]

No matter how many times I read it, Swami Vivekananda's address, and especially its concluding words, still sends chills up and down my spine. Tragically, his hopes for the end of fanaticism and bigotry have not been realized. But what a hope! It is a hope that is no less relevant today than when it was expressed at the first Parliament of the World's Religions on a late summer day in Chicago in 1893. Vivekananda's audacity is evident from the outset. In his greeting, "Sisters and Brothers of America," Vivekananda does not speak as a victim, a member of an oppressed

---

2. Swami Vivekananada, *Complete Works, Volume One* (Kolkata: Advaita Ashrama, 1979), 3–4.

nation whose independence from Western rule remained over half a century in the future. Nor is he at all apologetic about being a representative of a "pagan" or "heathen" religion, beyond the realm of Christianity. At the same time, he does not castigate the West for its imperialism or for its sense of its own superiority.[3] His tone is neither servile nor defiant, but calmly assertive. He addresses his audience as an equal, and with gratitude for the warmth with which many had, indeed, received him during his time in the United States (though he had also faced, and would continue to face, racism and ridicule from others throughout the course of his travels). It is also significant that he addresses his audience as "Sisters and Brothers" and not the more common "Brothers and Sisters." Women played a major role in supporting Vivekananda's mission throughout his time in the West, and he did not regard them as in any way inferior to men. This was twenty-seven years before women were granted the right to vote in the United States.

The message was clear to his audience, who received it with resounding applause. Some contemporary accounts claim that after these words, "Sisters and Brothers of America," the audience applauded for several minutes.

Vivekananda quickly turns to the issue of tolerance, certainly a desirable goal in a world full of intolerance. For Vivekananda, though, it is insufficient. Acceptance, rather than tolerance, is the goal for which he claims humanity should strive, and that he believes his own tradition has, in its best moments, proclaimed and embodied. "I am proud to belong to a religion which has taught the world both tolerance and universal acceptance. We believe not only in universal toleration, but we accept all religions as true." Elaborating further on this theme in a later speech,

---

3. Though he would do so in later lectures and writings over the course of his brief career.

Vivekananda says, quite bluntly, of tolerance that, "...so-called toleration is often blasphemy, and I do not believe in it." Vivekananda does not believe in toleration? "I believe in acceptance. Why should I tolerate? Toleration means that I think that you are wrong and I am just allowing you to live. Is it not a blasphemy to think that you and I are allowing others to live? I accept all religions that were in the past, and worship with them all...Not only shall I do all these, but I shall keep my heart open for all that may come in the future. Is God's book finished? Or is it still a continuous revelation going on?"[4]

As historical examples of this ideal of acceptance in practice, Vivekananda cites the fact that religious refugees, both Jewish and Zoroastrian, were welcomed in ancient India when they faced persecution in other lands. He also cites Hindu scriptures in which the ideal is expressed that all paths lead to the same ultimate goal. From the *Shiva Mahimna Stotra*, "As the different streams having their sources in different places all mingle their water in the sea, so, O Lord, the different paths which men take through different tendencies, various though they appear, crooked or straight, all lead to Thee." And from the *Bhagavad Gita*: "Whosoever comes to Me, through whatsoever form, I reach him; all men are struggling through paths which in the end lead to me." This is the authoritative religious basis, from a Hindu perspective, for acceptance of people of all religions. It is not a case of "Hate the sin, love the sinner." It is not that the inherent dignity of a human being outweighs a person's false beliefs, thus requiring that person to be accepted in spite of his or her beliefs. It is certainly not "tolerance." It is that the religions themselves have an inherent

---

4. Swami Vivekananda, "The Way to the Realisation of a Universal Religion" (delivered in the Universalist Church, Pasadena, California, January 28, 1900), *Complete Works: Volume Two* (Kolkata: Advaita Ashrama, 1979), 374.

value, that, despite the various contradictions and, yes, imperfections in religious belief systems and practices, all serve to manifest the divinity within humanity. They are thus to be not merely tolerated but positively respected and valued. This ideal is ancient in India, where it was expressed famously not only in the Hindu scriptures but in a public proclamation by the Emperor Ashoka: "One should listen to and respect the doctrines professed by others...All should be well-learned in the good doctrines of other religions...for all of them desire self-control and purity of heart."[5] One might note that many teachers of Asian traditions who came to the West in Swami Vivekananda's time—and these included many of those who shared the stage with him at the Parliament—had a strong universalist emphasis in their teaching. This was likely seen both as a counter to the exclusivist claims of many Christian missionaries, but also as a way of affirming, in an age in which scientific rationalism was ascendant, that the principles of these traditions were, like scientific principles, available to all reasonable persons and not the preserve of blind faith in a particular text or teacher.

Vivekananda concludes with a reflection on how far humanity has been, and how far we remain, from embodying the ideal of acceptance. "Sectarianism, bigotry, and its horrible descendant, fanaticism, have long possessed this beautiful earth. They have filled the earth with violence, drenched it often and often with human blood, destroyed civilisation and sent whole nations to despair. Had it not been for these horrible demons, human society would be far more advanced than it is now." These lines always bring to my mind Carl Sagan's assertion that, had the great library of Alexandria not been burned to the ground by a fanatical mob,

---

5. Aśokan Rock Edicts Numbers 7 and 12. S. Dhammika, *The Edicts of King Asoka*, http://www.accesstoinsight.org/lib/authors/dhammika/wheel386.html.

it is likely that humanity would be traveling to the stars by now. They are also a sobering reminder to all people of faith of the destruction and violence in which religion is so often implicated.

One might certainly ask why, if the vision that Vivekananda outlines in this address is the Hindu ideal, so much violence has been perpetrated in the last century not only by some adherents of traditions that emphasize exclusive adherence to only one path but also by some Hindus, who might be expected to be more pluralistic. Of course, another figure that took great inspiration from Vivekananda's teaching was Mohandas K. Gandhi, who in fact tried to visit the Swami on his deathbed during a visit to Kolkata for a meeting of the Indian National Congress.[6] Swami Vivekananda can certainly be cited as one of the sources of inspiration for the nonviolent branch of the movement for Indian independence, led by Gandhi. Tragically, however, neither Swami Vivekananda's inspiration nor Mahatma Gandhi's leadership was sufficient to diminish the mutual suspicions of many Hindus and Muslims during this era, suspicions very often instigated and exploited by the British policy of divide-and-rule and that led to the violence of the partition of India and Pakistan and the assassination of Gandhi by a fellow Hindu. Some have even argued that in making the case that Hindus should take pride in their great heritage of acceptance, Vivekananda inadvertently fueled what would emerge in later decades as Hindu nationalism, a right-wing movement that paradoxically uses the very fact of Hindu acceptance as an argument for Hindu superiority.[7] This may be an unfair assessment, given that Vivekananda was arguing not from a position of Hindu strength as a representative of the majority tradition

---

6. Joseph Lelyveld, *Great Soul: Mahatma Gandhi and His Struggle with India* (New York: Alfred A. Knopf, 2011), 50–51.

7. See, for example, Jyotirmaya Sharma, *Hindutva: Exploring the Idea of Hindu Nationalism* (New Delhi: Penguin India, 2006).

in a democratic country, but as a colonized subject of a Christian empire in which Hindu traditions had been subjected to enormous distortion and ridicule. However, the assumption that any one community is wholly innocent and inherently incapable of straying from its ideals is a dangerous and, all too often, a deadly one. Were Vivekananda to speak today, I believe he would affirm the Hindu ideal as strongly as he did in his lifetime as a universal ideal to which all human beings should aspire, but equally affirm that Hindus are as capable as anyone of falling prey to the lower impulses of fear, greed, and hatred, which are, as the *Bhagavad Gita* states, the true enemies of humanity.

There is reason to believe that this hope is well-founded. In the concluding lines of his address, Vivekananda expresses his wish that "the bell that tolled this morning in honour of this convention may be the death-knell of all fanaticism, of all persecutions with the sword or with the pen, and of all uncharitable feelings between persons wending their way to the same goal." "Sectarian, fanaticism, and bigotry" are the real objects of his criticism, and not any particular religious tradition or community. All communities are able to affirm the ideal of universal acceptance, even if they may arrive at it through a wide array of theological avenues. The problem is not diversity itself, but rather the "uncharitable feelings between persons wending their way to the same goal," the fears and suspicions among communities, all of whom would ultimately benefit from a world of mutual loving acceptance.

QUESTIONS FOR REFLECTION/DISCUSSION

1. How different is the world today from the world of Swami Vivekananda's time? Has humanity progressed since 1893 toward Vivekananda's ideal of universal acceptance?

2. Even if we grant Swami Vivekananda's claim that acceptance is superior to tolerance, is this realistic? Is it better to work in stages, from tolerance to acceptance? Or is the idea of tolerance inherently flawed?

3. Is it necessary to accept the beliefs of others as, on some level, true in order to accept them as people? Is there a stage between the "mere tolerance" that Swami Vivekananda rejects and the total acceptance that he teaches?

4. Is it possible to separate religion from the violence carried out in its name? To what extent are our religious teachings the problem, and to what extent is it an issue of human weakness?

FOR FURTHER READING

"After 150 Years, the Voice of Vivekananda Still Resounds." *Hinduism Today.* http://www.hinduismtoday.com/modules/smart section/ item.php?itemid=5344.

Christopher Isherwood. *Ramakrishna and His Disciples*. Hollywood, CA: Vedanta Press, 1965.

Swami Vivekananda. *Complete Work*s. Kolkata: Advaita Ashrama, 1979. Also available online at http://cwsw.belurmath.org.

Pravrajika Vrajaprana. *Vedanta: A Simple Introduction*. Hollywood, CA: Vedanta Press, 1999.

19

Nostra Aetate:
Catholic Charter for Interreligious Engagement

Ruben L. F. Habito

The Second Vatican Council (Vatican II) was the twenty-first ecumenical council of the Catholic Church in its two millennia of history. Held over a period of four years from 1962 to 1965, it can be considered a watershed in the history of the Roman Catholic Church since the time of the Reformation.[1]

Vatican II was convened by Pope John XXIII and continued by his successor Paul VI after the former's death on June 3, 1963. Vatican II took on the task of reexamining the role of the Church in the light of developments in the modern world. In an address launching the second phase of the sessions on September 29, 1963, Pope Paul VI delineated four specific objectives for the Council:

1. to define more clearly the nature of the Church and the role of its pastoral leaders, the bishops;

2. to renew the Church in the light of its founding inspiration in the Gospel message;

---

1. The last ecumenical council previous to Vatican II was held from 1868 to 1870 in Vatican City and is appropriately termed Vatican I. Previous to that was the Council of Trent, which took place in the wake of the Reformation and was held from 1545 to 1563.

3. to seek unity among Christians and seek pardon for Catholic responsibility in bringing about rifts and divisions; and

4. to initiate a dialogue with the contemporary world on different levels.

As its overall outcome, Vatican II issued four constitutions (authoritative documents proclaiming the fundamental position of the Catholic Church with regard to its nature and internal structure), three declarations (statements on a proper Catholic understanding of key thematic issues), and nine decrees (directives related to specific pastoral tasks), laying out guidelines for Catholics all over the world on different aspects of their individual and social lives in the light of their faith.

Nostra Aetate (also called the Declaration on Non-Christian Religions), the shortest among all the sixteen documents from Vatican II, belongs to the second category, and can be rightly called a Catholic Magna Carta (used in a loose and analogous sense) for interfaith relations, in that it is a landmark charter encouraging and supporting Catholic ventures in interreligious dialogue that are creative and forward-looking. Complemented by a correlative Declaration on Religious Freedom (*Dignitatis Humanae*), which assured as sacrosanct the respect for the individual's right to hold on to religious truth as guided by one's own conscience, affirmed as an inalienable God-given right, it enjoined Catholics to seek whatever is true and holy that may be found in other religions, and to acknowledge these as coming from the same God the Father of us all and who is the author of all that is true and holy. It thus overturned previously held attitudes based on a very restrictive interpretation of a doctrinal statement held since early church times, expressed in the dictum *extra ecclesiam, nulla salus* (outside the [Roman Catholic] Church there is no salvation), a way of thinking that all those who remain outside the Catholic Church do not have access to saving truth and are thus destined to perdition.

Overturning such exclusivist views dominant among Catholics in the pre–Vatican II era, which easily tended to be linked with attitudes of condescension, if not triumphalism and arrogance vis-à-vis people of other faiths, *Nostra Aetate* encouraged the Catholic faithful to study and learn from other religions, listing specific themes that Catholics may view with respect and admiration as found in the teachings and practices of different faith traditions of the world.

A specific and very important point that *Nostra Aetate* highlighted is that the Jewish people taken as a whole are not to be charged with or blamed for the death of Jesus. It rejected and condemned any form of persecution against Jews, including attitudes and expressions of anti-Semitism in any place and any time.[2]

Since its promulgation in the final weeks of the Council on October 28, 1965, *Nostra Aetate* has served as a mandate and guideline for ongoing engagement by Catholics in interreligious dialogue and cooperative work with people of different faiths, encouraging Catholics to actively reach out to and learn from other religious traditions in a way that may shed light on and enhance their theological understanding and spiritual life as Catholics.

Nostra Aetate Text (Excerpts)[3]

1. In our time, when day by day humankind is being drawn closer together, and the ties between different

---

2. It is worthy of mention that the original intent for this document was to re-examine and reconsider Catholic relations with the Jewish tradition and came to be expanded to include the question of engagement with other religions as the drafting process unfolded.

3. Adapted and revised for style and inclusive language from the English translation

peoples are becoming stronger, the Church examines more closely her relationship to non-Christian religions. In her task of promoting unity and love among human beings, indeed among nations, she considers above all in this declaration what human beings have in common and what draws them to fellowship.

All peoples are of one community, and one their origin, for God made the whole human race to live on the face of the earth. They have one final goal, God, whose providence, manifestations of goodness, and saving design extend to all people, until that time when the elect will be united in the Holy City, the city ablaze with the glory of God, where the nations will walk in God's light.

From the various religions, human beings expect answers to the unsolved riddles of the human condition, which today, even as in former times, deeply stir the hearts of all: What is it to be a human being? What is the meaning, the aim of our life? What is moral good, what is sin? Whence suffering and what purpose does it serve? Which is the road to true happiness? What are death, judgment and retribution after death? What, finally, is that ultimate inexpressible mystery which encompasses our existence: whence do we come, and where are we going?

2. From ancient times down to the present, there is found among various peoples a certain perception of that hidden power which hovers over the course of things and over the events of human history; at times some indeed have come to the recognition of a Supreme Being, or even of a Father. This perception and recognition penetrates their lives with a profound religious sense.

---

found on the Vatican webpage, http://www.vatican.va/archive/hist_councils/ii_vatican_council/documents/vat-ii_decl_19651028_nostra-aetate_en.html.

Religions...that are bound up with an advanced culture have struggled to answer the same questions by means of more refined concepts and a more developed language...religions found everywhere try to counter the restlessness of the human heart, each in its own manner, by proposing "ways," comprising teachings, rules of life, and sacred rites.

The Catholic Church rejects nothing that is true and holy in these religions. She regards with sincere reverence those ways of conduct and of life, those precepts and teachings which, though differing in many aspects from the ones she holds and sets forth, nonetheless often reflect a ray of that Truth which enlightens all human beings.

Indeed, she proclaims, and ever must proclaim Christ "the way, the truth, and the life" (John 14:6), in whom men and women may find the fullness of religious life, in whom God has reconciled all things.

The Church, therefore, exhorts her sons and daughters, that through dialogue and collaboration with the followers of other religions, carried out with prudence and love and in witness to the Christian faith and life, they recognize, preserve and promote the good things, spiritual and moral, as well as the values in their society and culture...

5. ... No foundation therefore remains for any theory or practice that leads to discrimination between human beings or people and people, so far as their human dignity and the rights flowing from it are concerned.

The Church reproves, as foreign to the mind of Christ, any discrimination against human beings, or harassment of them because of their race, color, condition of life, or religion...

Behind the formulation of *Nostra Aetate* were theological insights and developments that had been brewing for several decades, but were once held in suspicion by the dominant church authorities of the time. In particular, the works of Jesuits Henri de Lubac (1896–1991) and Karl Rahner (1904–1984), who were invited by their respective bishops as *periti* ("experts" who served as consultants on specific themes of the Council), stand out as major influences in the theological underpinnings of this declaration.

A key theme shared by these two giants of twentieth-century Catholic theology is the affirmation that everything in the created order (referred to as "nature" in theological tracts) is *as such* already suffused with divine grace, insofar as these are willed into existence by the same Source of love and grace, who "so loved the world as to send the only Begotten" (John 3:16). To see everything in this created universe as primordially suffused by divine grace is also to see each and every one as embraced by divine love and as included in the salvific will of God who draws all things to Godself. This is thus to acknowledge God's presence and saving action outside of the geographical, cultural, and historical parameters of the Catholic Church, a doctrinal position that was not characteristic of the catechetical teaching and culture of Catholicism in the pre–Vatican II period.

The hesitant and carefully phrased statement that "the Catholic Church rejects nothing that is true and holy in these religions" can be more boldly rephrased to say that whatever is true and holy in these other religions (and, by extension, whatever is true and holy whether referring to religion or not) originates from the One God who is Source of all that is true and holy. Catholics are enjoined to engage in "dialogue and collaboration with followers of other religions," and to "recognize and promote the good things, spiritual and moral, as well as the values in their society and culture" as features they may also welcome, learn from, and possibly incorporate in their very own way of life and way of thinking as Catholics.

This being said, an unmistakable and clear point of emphasis of *Nostra Aetate*, in line with the Catholic Church's unwavering tradition since early times, is that Catholics are called to proclaim, "and ever must proclaim Christ 'the way, the truth, and the life' (John 14:6), in whom men and women may find the fullness of religious life, in whom God has reconciled all things."

A thoughtful reader of *Nostra Aetate* will note two key points about which *Nostra Aetate* is emphatic, but which appear difficult to reconcile, or which may even seem to cancel each other out. First, there is the firm affirmation of all that is true and holy in other religions, with the accompanying exhortation for Catholics to engage people of other faiths in dialogue and collaboration with an attitude that recognizes, cherishes, and promotes those things found to be true and holy in those religions. Second, however, there is also a staunch emphasis that Catholics must continue to proclaim Christ as the Way, the Truth, and the Life to all with whom they engage in dialogue and collaboration.

If a Catholic/Christian enters into dialogue with people of other faiths with the overt or covert motivation of proclaiming Christ to them, this very attitude would undermine the sincerity and integrity of the dialogue process and reveal a lack of respect for what is true and holy in the other's religion. The non-Christian would-be partner in dialogue could readily be able to detect such an attitude, and this would prevent the dialogue from going any further in a genuine way. But conversely, if a Christian engages people of other faiths in a way that ignores or sets aside the mandate to "proclaim Christ as the Way, the Truth, and the Life," such an approach would fall short of the one's own integrity and fidelity to the Christian tradition.

In addressing this dilemma, it is relevant here to step back and consider the basics of the Christian faith tradition. The affirmation that Jesus Christ is both fully human *and* fully divine, that God is both One *and* Three, are fundamental tenets upon which the entire Christian faith tradition stands. In the debates among Christians through the centuries, the upholding of *both* scripture *and* tradition, of faith *and* reason as authoritative sources for Christian discernment, of the balance between salvific grace *and* works,[4] are examples of this *both-and* approach that is a hallmark of catholicity.[5] In short, holding apparent polar opposites in creative tension offers Catholics a way to move forward on the two-pronged dilemma of relating to other religious traditions.

The meaning of "proclaiming Christ" is what is in question here. If one takes this to mean an attempt to convince the dialogue partner(s) of the truth of one's own Christian faith over against the other's faith tradition, or to convert the other(s) to one's own side, this itself would betray the intent of the dialogue and subvert the entire process right from the start. But if one understands this mandate as one of "putting on the mind of Christ," invoking and embodying the very presence of the Risen One in the midst of our human encounters, this would call for an act of genuine self-emptying, as Christ "emptied himself" (Philippians 2:7), and being totally present in a Christ-like way in engaging in the dialogical encounter with the religious other.[6] One thus opens one's heart and mind and entire being to listening, learning

---

4. The age-old Lutheran-Catholic debate on the question of justification (grace vs. works) has concluded with mutual understanding on the matter. See Margaret O'Gara, "Lutherans and Catholics: Ending an Old Argument," *Commonweal* 127 (January 14, 2000): 8–9.

5. See Charles Curran, *Loyal Dissent: Memoir of a Catholic Theologian* (Washington, DC: Georgetown University Press, 2007), 190–93.

6. See John P. Keenan, *The Emptied Christ of Philippians: Mahāyāna Meditations* (Eugene, OR: Wipf and Stock, 2015).

from, walking with, and entering into the world of the religious other, and in doing so, being genuinely transformed in the process.

What this transformation might entail in concrete and existential terms would be unique and different for every person who engages in this encounter. Theologians would find untold treasures that would open up exciting new dimensions in Christian ways of being and thinking, as they pursue their work of doing Christian theology.[7] Socio-ecologically engaged Christians would find allies and partners among those belonging to other religious communities and traditions while receiving inspiration and renewed empowerment from them as they together dedicate their lives to take on the enormous tasks of healing our wounded Earth community.[8] Christian seekers would find a rich mine of resources in the spiritual practices of other traditions that would enhance and deepen their own Christian spiritual life.[9]

In sum, *Nostra Aetate* can be regarded as a pivotal historic document that unleashed new initiatives and opened new horizons in interreligious engagement among Catholics, as well as other Christians, giving theological grounding and ecclesiastical support to the vital endeavors that continue to bear abundant fruit in our contemporary multi-faith global community, as those of us

---

7. The emerging field of comparative theology, involving more and more Christian scholars and thinkers delving deeply into texts and traditions of other religious traditions with an attitude of respect and humble learning, is now opening new and exciting horizons for Christian self-understanding and praxis. See, for example, Francis Clooney, ed., *The New Comparative Theology: Interreligious Insights from the Next Generation* (London: Bloomsbury T&T Clark, 2010), and the bibliographical list therein.

8. See, for example, the chapter on "Buddhist-Christian Socially Engaged Dialogue," in Paul Ingram, *The Process of Buddhist-Christian Dialogue* (Eugene, OR: Cascade Books, 2009), 83–102.

9. See the classic work by the late Anthony de Mello, SJ, *Sadhana: Way to God: Christian Exercises in Eastern Form* (New York: Image Books, 1984); Susan J. Stabile, *Growing in Love and Wisdom: Tibetan Buddhist Sources for Christian Meditation* (New York: Oxford University Press, 2012); and Ellen Birx, *Selfless Love: Beyond the Boundaries of Self and Other* (Boston: Beacon Press, 2014) as excellent examples of what has been termed "interspiritual dialogue."

who identify as members of the different religious traditions as well as those of no religion together take up our immense tasks of working toward our shared future.

QUESTIONS FOR REFLECTION/DISCUSSION

1. How would you compare the attitudes of Catholics vis-à-vis people of other faiths in the pre–Vatican II era with those after *Nostra Aetate*?

2. What are some theological grounds provided by *Nostra Aetate* for Catholics and other Christians to engage with those in other religious traditions with respect and an attitude of openness?

3. Is it possible to reconcile the tension apparent in *Nostra Aetate* between the encouragement to recognize and promote what is true and holy in other traditions and the mandate to "proclaim Christ as the Way, the Truth, and the Life"?

4. How can the mandate to "proclaim Christ" be understood and enacted in a way that does not betray or diminish the Christian integrity and sincerity required in the dialogue with religious others?

FOR FURTHER READING

David Brockman and Ruben L.F. Habito, eds. *The Gospel among Religions: Christian Ministry, Theology, and Spirituality in a Multifaith World*. Maryknoll, NY: Orbis Books, 2010.

Henri de Lubac. *The Mystery of the Supernatural (Milestones in Catholic Theology)*. New York: Crossroads, 1998.

James Fredericks. *Faith Among Faiths: Christianity and the Other Religions*. Mahwah, NJ: Paulist Press, 1999.

Karl Rahner. "Christianity and Non-Christian Religions." In *Theological Investigations Vol. 5: Later Writings*, 118–34. Translated by Karl-H. Kruger. Baltimore, MD: Helicon, 1966.

20

"Whatever Pleases the One"

Guru Nanak's Response to Violence and Warfare

RAHULDEEP GILL

This particular hymn from the Guru Granth Sahib, or Sikh scripture, grips its audience by juxtaposing a description of feminine beauty with the brutality of war, especially for war's civilian victims. All 1,430 pages of the Guru Granth Sahib contain divinely inspired poetry of many of the Gurus, or Sikh founding figures. The Guru Granth Sahib is unique among world scriptures because it also contains the poems of Hindu and Muslim poets whose theologies resonated with the Sikh ethos. This hymn brings to the fore the plight of innocent Hindu and Muslim civilians who have been viciously ravaged by war.

The hymn also fascinates me because it is a clear instance of a world historical event that we can locate in the life of the Sikh founder, and first Guru, Baba ("Father") Nanak (1469–1539). The events described in this hymn would have taken place in the early 1520s when the Turkic-Mongol invader, and eventual founder of the Mughal dynasty and empire, Babur, entered al-Hind, in northwest India. Thus, the hymn captures not only the violence of invasion but also the deeply destabilizing transfer of power from the Sultanate of the Lodi Afghans to the burgeoning empire of Babur's Mughal clan. This would not be the last violent encounter between the Mughal empire and the Sikh community. In the next two centuries, two Sikh Gurus (the fifth, Guru Arjan in 1606, and the ninth, Guru Tegh Bahadur in 1675) would be brutally executed on personal orders from Mughal emperors.

From early stories about his life, we know that Guru Nanak was a politically connected religious prophet. He is said to have begun his career as an accountant working under the auspices of Daulat Khan, a Lodi noble who would turn against the Sultanate and encourage Babur to invade al-Hind. Rewarded under Mughal rule for his invitation to Babur, Daulat Khan would eventually rise to the rank of governor of Punjab, which is the administrative region where Sikhism was born and still thrives. What could it mean in Guru Nanak's life that someone of such great power was his mentor, and perhaps his one-time patron? What did it mean for Guru Nanak that such a person as Daulat Khan Lodi was partly responsible for the deaths of innocents that are described in this hymn? Guru Nanak's own compositions do not directly address this looming question.

The hymn is one of four that fall under the category of *Babur Bani*, or hymns about Babur's invasion. In these hymns, Guru Nanak takes prophetic aim at the brutally violent invasion and the political games that kings and nobles play for which innocent lives are sacrificed. These hymns are interpreted in different ways by Sikh preachers. Some believe that Guru Nanak is not only castigating Babur in these hymns, but that Baba is also questioning God's plan in a violently unjust world.

Braids in their locks,
    vermillion in their scalp,
Their heads were shorn with scissors
    and dust fell into their mouths.

They used to live in mansions
    and now find no place to rest.

Hail, Baba! Hail the Primal Being!
Your end cannot be found,
    You create and behold
        Your own guise.

When they were wed,
    their grooms by their sides,
Arriving in palanquins
    decked with ivory,

    water was poured out for their good.[1]
They were cooled by fans inlaid with glass.

They received millions in blessings when they sat
    and millions when they stood.
They ate coconuts. They ate dates.
    They enjoyed their beds.
Then ropes were placed around their necks
    breaking their garlands of pearls.

Wealth and youth, which had given them such joy,
    then became their enemies,
When soldiers were given the command
    to take their honor and carry them off.
When the One pleases—greatness.
    When the One pleases—punishment.

But why should they have been punished
    if they had thought of the One before?

---

1. In Punjabi wedding cultures, a bowl of water is waved around the head of new-lyweds to capture any bad spirits they may have attracted. The water is poured out or drunk by a relative.

It was the kings who lost their minds
    reveling in pleasure and sport,
It was Babur's word that spread through the land
    when even princes could not find a morsel.

Some lost their five prayers,
    and others lost their *puja*-worship.
Hindu women, having lost their cooking squares,
    can't affix their marriage marks.
Having never remembered Ram
    they can't find "Khuda" to chant.

Some found their homes again
    and some found their inquiring families.
Some found only this in their writ:
    to cry out in suffering.
Whatever pleases the One happens,
    Nanak, what are humans?

I do not think that Guru Nanak assumes here that God has sent punishment upon the innocent women mentioned in this hymn. He depicts scenes of disaster that have unfolded around him. The pervasive problem with the way they have unfolded is that those who will themselves to power lack any and all God-consciousness. These leaders fail to accept that all human life is precious, and therefore, they cause unthinkable suffering and carnage. But their God-fearing subjects are left with perpetual questions in the face of this man-made suffering. *Why?* Why is such brutality possible? Why do men demonstrate their power over and upon the bodies of women? Why did this happen in the 1520s? Why was there large-scale violence against women again in 1947 when India and Pakistan were partitioned under the rule of the outgoing British Empire? Why are women and girls kidnapped? Why does sex trafficking remain a thriving industry?

There are three aims that Guru Nanak, as the founding teacher of a great world religion, accomplishes with this hymn. First, he builds resonance with other hymns about the fragility of life, making divine remembrance absolutely necessary. Second, he bewails the invader, Babur, and kings like him, who play games with the lives of the innocent. Third, he calls out to God for justice from the perspective of the powerless human—Muslim, Hindu, or Sikh—who beholds injustice tearing the world apart. Alas, he seems to conclude, anticipating Matthew Arnold in "Dover Beach," human existence is like that of pebbles in the sand,

> *. . . here as on a darkling plain*
> *Swept with confused alarms of struggle and flight,*
> *Where ignorant armies clash by night.*

But Guru Nanak is not a pessimist or a nihilist. In fact, he believes a life of deep meaning is possible for those whose intentions are right, those who seek to engage all of God's creation with care and consideration. Indeed, for Guru Nanak, intention, godliness, and working for the common good are inseparable.

He also stresses the fact that life could end at any moment and that too many of us forget this fact, especially those of us who live comfortably. But remembering death is an essential part of Guru Nanak's spiritual prescriptions:

> Remember the Master,
> brothers, we all will walk this path.
> Our work here is but for a few days, and we are certain
>   to depart.

We are certain to depart, as guests do,
so why take pride?
There is One who we can serve and find peace hereafter.
We should call on only that One.
Hereafter, our way will sway no one, only what we have
    done will matter, so
Remember the Master,
brothers, we all will walk this path.

                                   —Guru Granth Sahib, p. 479

Guru Nanak emphasizes throughout his compositions that those who have harmed others in this life will be punished in the next life and will find no place in God's presence. Those who have lived selflessly and given their lives to divine remembrance will be exalted. Divine remembrance is, therefore, no mere contemplative exercise for Guru Nanak, but a deeply ethical matter. Only those who have acted in this world with attention to service find a place in the hereafter.

Guru Nanak compares Babur, whose name means "tiger," to a wild beast who preys on innocent, plant-eating herds. Elsewhere, Guru Nanak writes that all kings are tigers, and their officials are carrion-eating dogs who live off the flesh of others (Guru Granth Sahib, p. 1288):

Deer, hawks, and politicians
are known to be clever
For they set traps that trap their own!
They will find no place hereafter.

It seems for Guru Nanak that tyrants and murderers will find their ultimate punishment at the moment of death, when they meet their Maker. But what hope is there in *this* life to be rid of such injustice?

Justice is a constant theme in Guru Nanak's poetry: who is responsible, God or humans? On the one hand, it seems that if humans were to attune themselves to the *hukam* (God's will), cultivate a relationship with the Divine, and stay away from their selfish natures, then the world would be much better. But then elsewhere, he also seems to suggest that that the strife of life is part of the divine plan. If God wanted, Nanak suggests, the world could be different.

These issues seem to always be in paradoxical tension. Guru Nanak is unquestionably sensitive to the injustice of the world, which can result in a sense of alienation and despair. Perhaps the tension can be resolved if we understand that God does not "create" the strife because God is cruel or insensitive, but that God's agency in the world is different, more mysterious, than what we might wish it to be. Does God have the power to change things? Yes. But the *hukam* is unfolding as it should, and it includes allowing for human free will and agency (good and bad). But what about illnesses or natural disasters that are simply beyond our control? Life sometimes sucks. Humans are tiny beings. God knows what's what. Perhaps the difference between the agnostic and the Sikh is simply commitment to a religious path, even as painful questions about the nature of evil (theodicy) remain.

In my life, I do two kinds of interreligious work: civic and political. In my civic work, I cannot engage only with those people with whom I agree on religious or political matters. This kind of work necessitates working across various ideological lines, and it includes working with individuals who have different definitions of justice and differing commitments to justice. In this sphere, I must engage with such people so that our cities, towns, and neighborhoods are coated with the civic glue that keeps potholes filled, schools running, the homeless fed, and partisan debates from spilling into violence.

In the other kind of interfaith work that I do, I engage with people with different religious (and secular) convictions for the purpose of advancing my progressive political agenda. As is the case with my civic interreligious engagement, I find inspiration and guidance for this work from my faith tradition, which teaches me that I should stand up and be in solidarity with those who proclaim that "Black Lives Matter." These values demand that I work not just to feed the homeless but also to publicly question the systemic oppression that keeps people homeless in the first place. These values demand that I challenge hatred, bigotry, and injustice not only in its most overt forms but also when it is manifest more shrewdly in the abuse of undocumented workers, the disenfranchisement of minority voters, and the degradation of the lands of indigenous communities through drilling and the like.

The two kinds of interreligious work that I do are often in tension with each other. To achieve civic harmony, I have to work with people whose ideas of justice challenge my vision of justice. To achieve a more equitable world, I have to sometimes work directly against my partners in interreligious civic engagement.

The sacred teachings of my Sikh tradition, such as the ones I have shared, give me the inspiration and patience to tease out this challenge. Exploring the ways in which figures like Guru Nanak and other visionaries responded to human suffering with courage and compassion—within both the civic and political realms—helps me persevere in my own attempts to produce positive change across religious and other lines of difference. The Gurus' profound understanding that all of life is invested with divinity, and that we must treat people from different religious and cultural traditions with dignity, grounds me when engaging with allies and opponents alike. Finally, the openness of the Sikh founders as well as their willingness to learn from and honor other sources of wisdom humbles me daily, especially when grappling with such complex questions of God's presence in human history and our capacity to live justly and peacefully.

QUESTIONS FOR REFLECTION/DISCUSSION

1. How do you understand the relationship between human free will and God's will? If these terms do not resonate with you, how do you think about such terms as fate or destiny, karma, or chance and randomness?

2. Is the subject of "theodicy," of God's goodness and the existence of evil, a significant issue in your life? To what extent do teachings from your religious tradition help you address this issue?

3. Do you experience any tension between civic and political forms of interreligious engagement? Are you drawn to one form more than the other? If so, why?

FOR FURTHER READING

Rahuldeep Gill. *Drinking from Love's Cup: Surrender and Sacrifice in the Vars of Bhai Gurdas Bhalla.* New York: Oxford University Press, 2016.

Eleanor Nesbitt. *Sikhism: A Very Short Introduction.* New York: Oxford University Press, 2005.

21

Spiritual Activism

Abraham Joshua Heschel's Telegram to President Kennedy

OR N. ROSE

On June 16, 1963, Abraham Joshua Heschel (1907–1972) sent the following telegram to President John F. Kennedy. Rabbi Heschel timed his challenging message to arrive just one day before the two were scheduled to meet in person at a national gathering of religious leaders at the White House. The purpose of the meeting was to discuss African American civil rights. Ever the spiritual and ethical gadfly, Heschel hoped that this brief, but sharply worded letter would stir JFK and the assembled clergy to take bold action against segregation and not settle for more "solemn" declarations. While Heschel issued a searing critique of U.S. Jewish and Christian leaders in this telegram, he did so believing strongly in the power of such interreligious alliances to make significant change in the world.

TO PRESIDENT JOHN F. KENNEDY, THE WHITE HOUSE, JUNE 16, 1963. I LOOK FORWARD TO PRIVILEGE OF BEING PRESENT AT MEETING TOMORROW AT FOUR P.M. LIKELIHOOD EXISTS THAT NEGRO PROBLEM WILL BE LIKE THE WEATHER. EVERYBODY TALKS ABOUT IT BUT

NOBODY DOES ANYTHING ABOUT IT. PLEASE DEMAND OF RELIGIOUS LEADERS PERSONAL INVOLVEMENT NOT JUST SOLEMN DECLARATION. WE FORFEIT RIGHT TO WORSHIP GOD AS LONG AS WE CONTINUE TO HUMILI-ATE NEGROES. CHURCH SYNAGOGUE HAVE FAILED. THEY MUST REPENT. ASK OF RELIGIOUS LEADERS TO CALL FOR NATIONAL REPENTANCE AND PERSONAL SACRIFICE. LET RELIGIOUS LEADERS DONATE ONE MONTH'S SALARY TOWARD FUND FOR NEGRO HOUSING AND EDUCATION. I PROPOSE THAT YOU MR. PRESIDENT DECLARE STATE OF MORAL EMERGENCY. A MARSHALL PLAN FOR AID TO NEGROES IS BECOMING A NECESSITY. THE HOUR CALLS FOR MORAL GRANDEUR AND SPIRITUAL AUDACITY.[1]

Abraham Joshua Heschel came to the United States in 1940, having narrowly escaped the brutal Nazi onslaught in Europe. Born in Warsaw, Poland, into an illustrious Hasidic family, Heschel was a graduate student at the University of Berlin and at the Reform rabbinical school when Hitler came to power in 1933. After being deported to Poland in 1938, Heschel received a special scholar's visa from Hebrew Union College in Cincinnati, Ohio. He left Warsaw in 1939, just six weeks before Germany invaded Poland. Many of Heschel's family members—including his mother and three of his sisters—were murdered by the Nazis in the following months and years. In reflecting on this agonizing

---

1. Dr. Susannah Heschel, daughter of Abraham Joshua Heschel, first published this telegram in *Moral Grandeur and Spiritual Audacity: Essays* (New York: Farrar, Straus and Giroux, 1996), vii. A photograph of the original document can be viewed on the website of the Jewish Women's Archive, http://jwa.org/media/telegram-from-abraham-joshua-heschel-to-president-john-f-kennedy-june-16-1963.

turn of events, he described himself as "a brand plucked from the fire in which my people were burned to death."[2]

After acculturating to life in the United States and establishing himself as a respected scholar and gifted religious writer, Heschel became increasingly involved in public affairs. This involvement included his engagement in the civil rights movement, the struggle for the religious and cultural freedom of Soviet Jews, the Second Vatican Council, and the protest movement against the war in Vietnam. It was no coincidence that Heschel emerged as a social activist as he was working on the English adaptation of his doctoral dissertation on the Hebrew prophets. Reflecting on the impact of this writing project on his life, Heschel said the following in an interview just weeks before he died in 1972:

I've written a book on the prophets. A rather large book. I spent many years [completing it]. And, really, this book changed my life. Because early in my life, my great love was for learning, studying. And the place where I preferred to live was my study and books and writing and thinking. I've learned from the prophets that I have to be involved in the affairs of man, in the affairs of suffering man.[3]

---

2. Abraham Joshua Heschel, "No Religion Is an Island," *Abraham Joshua Heschel: Essential Writings*, selected with an introduction by Susannah Heschel (Maryknoll, NY: Orbis Books, 2011), 116. Heschel first delivered this as a speech at Union Theological Seminary in 1965, where he served as the first Harry Emerson Fosdick Visiting Professor during the academic year 1965–1966. To learn more about Heschel's life in Europe, see Edward K. Kaplan and Samuel H. Dresner, *Abraham Joshua Heschel: Prophetic Witness* (New Haven, CT: Yale University Press, 1998).

3. "Carl Stern's Interview with Dr. Heschel," in *Moral Grandeur and Spiritual Audacity*, 399. This interview originally aired on NBC television on February 4, 1972, as part of the *Eternal Light* series of the Jewish Theological Seminary of America.

Heschel gave his first major address on civil rights in March 1963 at the inaugural Conference on Religion and Race in Chicago. In his remarks, he compared the plight of African Americans in the United States to that of the ancient Israelite slaves in Egypt. In one particularly dramatic moment, he stated, "In fact, it may have been easier for the Children of Israel to cross the Red Sea than for a Negro to cross certain university campuses."[4] He went on to challenge the audience—including Jews—to pick up Moses's mantle in an effort to uproot racism from American life.

It was at this conference that Heschel first met Dr. King. The two became close friends and colleagues and remained so until King's murder in 1968. While these men came from very different backgrounds, they shared several qualities that brought them together during a tumultuous and transformative period in American life. Both were born to prominent religious families and were groomed for leadership by their elders. Both were passionate believers in a God of compassion and righteousness, who called on humankind to serve as co-creators of a world suffused with these values. Each turned to the Bible and other sacred writings for inspiration and guidance while also employing various historical-critical methods of interpretation. And both were masterful at using their exegetical and linguistic skills to awaken people's consciousness and stir them to action. Finally, Heschel and King both understood the power of interfaith and cross-cultural relationships for personal growth *and* social transformation.[5]

---

4. Abraham Joshua Heschel, "Religion and Race," *Abraham Joshua Heschel: Essential Writings*, 65.

5. To learn more about the intellectual and religious dimensions of this historic relationship, see Susannah Heschel's essay, "Theological Affinities in the Writings of Abraham Joshua Heschel and Martin Luther King, Jr.," in *Black Zion: African American Religious Encounters with Judaism*, ed. Yvonne Chireau and Nathaniel Deutsch (New York: Oxford University Press), 168–86.

In our textual selection, Heschel writes in the same polemical tone he had used in his Chicago address earlier that same year. Here, however, his focus is specifically on the Jewish and Christian communities and their leaders. Heschel's critique is sharp and to the point (as a telegram demands): "We forfeit the right to worship God as long as we continue to humiliate Negros." In fine prophetic fashion, he rails against ritual observance divorced from social responsibility. As he writes elsewhere, "Prayer is no panacea, no substitute for action."[6] While Heschel was an eloquent spokesperson for a life of disciplined religious praxis—including prayer[7]—he was steadfast in his call for a holistic approach to spirituality and ethics. Importantly, in this telegram Heschel speaks explicitly about the relationship between racism, poverty, and education, going so far as to suggest that the president use his executive powers to proclaim a "state of moral emergency" and that a domestic version of the Marshall Plan[8] might be necessary to properly address the issue. In such troubled times, writes Heschel, it is all the more important that religious leaders actually *lead*—not only in word but also in deed. As a sign of their contrition and commitment to civil rights, he suggests that American clergy make a personal "sacrifice" of one month's salary.

Two years after writing this pointed telegram to JFK, Heschel joined Dr. King and other civil rights leaders in the historic Selma march. Upon returning from that protest he wrote the following words:

---

6. Abraham Joshua Heschel, *Man's Quest for God: Studies in Prayer and Symbolism* (New York: Charles Scribner's Sons, 1954), 8.

7. See, for example, *Man's Quest for God* and *The Sabbath: Its Meaning for Modern Man* (New York: Farrar, Straus and Giroux, 1951).

8. The Marshall Plan, named after Secretary of State George Marshall, was a thirteen billion dollar American initiative to help restore European economies after World War II; it is also known as the European Recovery Program.

For many of us the march from Selma to Montgomery was about protest and prayer. Legs are not lips and walking is not kneeling. And yet our legs uttered songs. Even without words, our march was worship. I felt my legs were praying.[9]

For Heschel, marching for voting rights was a holy act, an embodied devotional response to God's ongoing call for justice and compassion; his Hasidic forebears might have called it *avodah b'gashmiut*, "worship through corporeality." Interestingly, in this brief reflection he alternates between the singular and the plural, thus suggesting that this was a shared experience of worship ("even without words") among people from different religious traditions. In this same context, Heschel also wrote that marching with Dr. King and the other activists reminded him of walking with the great Hasidic masters of his youth. This was a powerful ecumenical statement in itself but even more remarkable when one considers Heschel's traumatic experiences of anti-Semitism and the negative portrayal of gentiles in many Hasidic teachings.[10] Rather than turn away from engagement with non-Jews in anger and despair, he became a champion for racial justice and interreligious cooperation.

---

9. While the statement "I felt my legs were praying" is well known and often quoted by Jewish leaders, I saw this fuller quotation for the first time in a recent television interview with Susannah Heschel conducted by Melissa Harris-Perry of MSNBC on March 8, 2015 in honor of the fiftieth anniversary of the Selma march, http://www.msnbc.com/melissa-harris-perry/watch/john-lewis-recounts-memories-of-bloody-sunday-410061379607. (Heschel commentary begins at 5:23 mark in recording.)

10. Part of Heschel's intellectual-spiritual project was to share with his readers the beauties of Hasidism, while also reshaping elements of it in light of his own and his readers' modern Western sensibilities. On this aspect of Heschel's work, see Arthur Green, "Abraham Joshua Heschel: Recasting Hasidism for Moderns," *Modern Judaism: A Journal of Jewish Ideas and Experience* 29, no. 1 (February 2009): 62–79.

In addition to his friendship with Dr. King, Heschel also cultivated relationships with several Christian scholars, theologians, and activists, including Reinhold Niebuhr, Thomas Merton, and William Sloane Coffin. He not only participated in public interfaith programs but also invested in *personal* relationships. Heschel possessed the confidence, curiosity, and trust to engage with his non-Jewish peers in serious and ongoing discussions of theology and religious experience, as well as moral and political matters.[11]

Of course, Heschel was also involved in various public interfaith initiatives, including, most famously, the Second Vatican Council (1962–1964). He played an important consultative role at various stages of these historic deliberations and in the crafting of the landmark document *Nostra Aetate* ("In Our Time"). During the academic year 1965–1966, Heschel held the inaugural Harry Emerson Fosdick Visiting Professorship at Union Theological Seminary. It was there that he wrote his most sustained reflection on interfaith cooperation, entitled "No Religion Is an Island." And in 1966 Heschel helped to found the interfaith organization Clergy Concerned about Vietnam (CCAV), serving as the first co-chair with Richard John Neuhaus and Daniel Berrigan. Heschel remained intensely involved in anti–Vietnam War efforts until his death in 1972.[12]

---

11. See Susannah Heschel's reflections on these relationships in her introduction to *Abraham Joshua Heschel: Essential Writings*, 28–34. Interestingly, in "No Religion Is an Island," Heschel warns his listeners that not all people are prepared intellectually or spiritually for such substantive interfaith discussions. See *Abraham Joshua Heschel: Essential Writings*, 124. As Alon Goshen Gottstein has observed, the international interfaith movement has evolved such that today many people with varying levels of knowledge and commitment are, in fact, involved in discussions of theology and spirituality. We can only wonder what Heschel might have thought of this and other developments in the movement. See Goshen Gottsein's article, "Heschel and Interreligious Dialogue—Formulating the Questions," in *Abraham Joshua Heschel: Philosophy, Theology, and Interreligious Dialogue*, ed. Stanislaw Krajewski and Adam Lipszyc (Wiesbaden, Germany: Harrasowitz Verlag, 2009), 161–67.

12. See Edward Kaplan's second volume of his biography of Heschel, *Spiritual*

As a rabbi committed to interreligious education and activism, I consider Abraham Joshua Heschel to be an important role model and a challenging presence in my life. Not only did he labor to revitalize Jewish spiritual life in the United States, he also played a distinctive role as a Jewish leader in several historic efforts to help heal racial, religious, and political wounds in the United States and the wider world. While Heschel wrote relatively little about interfaith engagement, the few pieces he did pen, along with his larger body of work on the ground, provide us rich material to grapple with and learn from as we seek to build upon his legacy. May Abraham Joshua Heschel's memory continue to serve as a source of inspiration to all who engage in the ongoing task of mending our beautiful and broken world.

QUESTIONS FOR REFLECTION/DISCUSSION

1. Compare Heschel's remarks about worship in his telegram to JFK with his reflection following the Selma march. How do these relate to each other?

2. Most of Heschel's interfaith interlocutors were Christian— Catholic and Protestant. With whom do you engage or wish to engage in such encounters? Why?

3. Heschel engaged in different forms of interreligious dialogue and action, including theological reflection, textual study, and social justice. What kinds of interfaith engagement do you think are most urgently needed today?

Radical: Abraham Joshua Heschel in America (New Haven, CT: Yale University Press, 2000).

FURTHER READING

Shai Held. *Abraham Joshua Heschel: The Call of Transcendence.* Bloomington, IN: Indiana University Press, 2013.

Abraham Joshua Heschel. *Abraham Joshua Heschel: Essential Writings*, selected with an introduction by Susannah Heschel. Maryknoll, NY: Orbis Books, 2011.

Abraham Joshua Heschel. *Between Man and God: An Interpretation of Judaism*, selected, edited, and introduced by Fritz A. Rothschild. New York: Harper & Row, 1959.

Abraham Joshua Heschel. *Moral Grandeur and Spiritual Audacity: Essays*, edited by Susannah Heschel. New York: Farrar, Straus, and Giroux, 2006.

Edward K. Kaplan. *Spiritual Radical: Abraham Joshua Heschel in America.* New Haven, CT: Yale University Press, 2000.

Michael Marmur. *Abraham Joshua Heschel and the Sources of Wonder.* Toronto: University of Toronto Press, 2016.

22

Archbishop Oscar Romero's Call for Peace and Reconciliation

MT DÁVILA

On March 23, 1980, Archbishop Oscar Romero preached what would be his last sermon to the people of El Salvador. Chosen for his reputation as a quiet intellectual, Romero was placed at the helm of the diocese of San Salvador in 1977, during one of the most brutal civil wars in Latin American history. While believing that the role of the clergy was to sustain the spiritual needs of the faithful through liturgy and sacraments, Romero could no longer ignore the ongoing human rights abuses by the military establishment, the violence of various resistance groups, and especially the persecution of church leaders—lay women and men as well as priests—who spoke out in favor of the rights of peasants and the dignity of the poor. He became an adamant advocate for human rights, speaking strongly against the alliance between the government, the landed gentry, and the military, and denouncing foreign intervention in El Salvador in the form of U.S. military aid to the country in the effort to hold communism at bay in Central America.

Romero would broadcast weekly addresses and sermons over the Catholic radio station, which was bombed on more than one occasion in efforts to silence his messages. He knew his life was in danger, but he continued to preach a message of hope to the poor and oppressed as well as a message of conversion to the military and the government. In this, his final broadcasted sermon, Romero once again catalogues the atrocities against the people —assassinations, wholesale attacks on villages—often mentioning the names of the victims, recalling their relations, placing them within the context of daily hopes for a fulfilling life. His cataloguing of injustices and human rights violations was a trademark of his messages, combining the realities of history with the messages of hope and liberation in the Jewish and Christian Bibles. Romero used his messages to appeal on behalf of the Salvadoran people to the United Nations, the United States government, and the highest Catholic authority at the Vatican.

The fissures that broke through the social, political, economic, and even religious landscape of El Salvador during these troubled years shattered the veneer of homogeneity of a mostly Roman Catholic population. Divisions of class and origin, especially between indigenous and/or poor peasants, landed aristocracy, and a military establishment that craftily gathered from all classes while serving the political elite alone, meant that there was no neutral position for the Catholic Church to take. Messages that promoted an otherworldly spirituality benefited the status quo, leaving unquestioned the oppressive excesses of the military and political elite. Romero's thought and preaching, and this sermon in particular, acknowledged these divisions and transcended them by summoning all listeners to come together under the affirmation of the dignity of all humanity to discern their part in creating a society free of violence where all could thrive and where power was shared across different dimensions of Salvadoran life. Romero was keenly aware of the weight of responsibility that befell one who would try to weave through these boundaries and fissures, mending relationships while clamoring for justice.

As a Catholic engaged in interfaith theological education, I find in Romero's example a witness to how the work of justice must mind perceived and real fractures among different groups, particularly among groups who rarely get invited to shared conversations on their political and social destiny. In particular, I am moved to uncover facile claims of unity or homogeneity that may veil deep discord on critical issues of justice at this time.

Romero's final homily, and the stern challenge to the military issued within the words cited below, is considered to be the message that finalized plans for his assassination. Romero was killed the next afternoon, while he was saying Mass at the chapel of the Hospital of Divine Mercy.

Let no one be offended because we use the divine words read at our mass to shed light on the social, political and economic situation of our people. Not to do so would be un-Christian. Christ desires to unite himself with humanity, so that the light he brings from God might become life for nations and individuals.

I know many are shocked by this preaching and want to accuse us of forsaking the gospel for politics. But I reject this accusation. I am trying to bring to life the message of the Second Vatican Council[1] and the meetings at Medellín and Puebla[2] ... Each week I go about the country listening to the cries of the people, their pain from so

1. The Second Vatican Council was a global meeting of Catholic bishops in Rome from 1962 to 1965. The resulting documents from this gathering were groundbreaking in many ways, perhaps most importantly because of the way the Council incorporated culture, history, and world religions into its considerations but also the centrality of the poor in its development. These documents are accessible in English at http:// www.vatican.va/archive/hist_councils /ii_vatican_council/index.htm.

2. The Latin American bishops had two general meetings in the critical years leading up to these events in the life of Archbishop Romero, one in Medellín (1968), and one in Puebla (1979). The full text (in Spanish) of the resulting documents can be found at http://www.celam.org/conferencias_generales.php.

much crime, and the ignominy of so much violence. Each week I ask the Lord to give me the right words to console, to denounce, to call for repentance...

Every country lives its own "exodus"; today El Salvador is living its own exodus. Today we are passing to our liberation through a desert strewn with bodies and where anguish and pain are devastating us. Many suffer the temptation of those who walked with Moses and wanted to turn back and did not work together. It is the same old story. God, however, wants to save the people by making a new history...

I would like to make a special appeal to the men of the army, and specifically to the ranks of the National Guard, the police and the military. Brothers, you come from our own people. You are killing your own brother peasants when any human order to kill must be subordinate to the law of God which says, "Thou shall not kill." No soldier is obliged to obey an order contrary to the law of God. No one has to obey an immoral law. It is high time you recovered your consciences and obeyed your consciences rather than a sinful order. The church, the defender of the rights of God, of the law of God, of human dignity, of the person, cannot remain silent before such an abomination. We want the government to face the fact that reforms are valueless if they are to be carried out at the cost of so much blood. In the name of God, in the name of this suffering people whose cries rise to heaven more loudly each day, I implore you, I beg you, I order you in the name of God: stop the repression.

The church preaches your liberation just as we have studied it in the holy Bible today. It is a liberation that has, above all else, respect for the dignity of the person, hope

for humanity's common good, and the transcendence
that looks before all to God and only from God derives its
hope and its strength.[3]

Romero's sermon came at the cusp of the Lenten season, a
few days before the beginning of the holiest season in the Christian calendar, when the faithful recall in liturgy and devotional
practices the arrest, trial, and crucifixion of Jesus, leading to the
celebration of his resurrection on Easter Sunday.[4] A week before,
Romero reached into the narrative of Passover in the book of Exodus, one understood by Christians as central to the life of Jesus
during the days leading to his arrest. The theme of liberation from
oppression by God's intervention throughout the Exodus story is
one that also speaks directly to the suffering that Romero witnessed among the people of El Salvador. Their persecution at the
hands of the government, the military, and the landowners knew
no limits at the time, when villages were attacked under the pre-
tense of harboring enemies of the state and villagers were round-
ed up and summarily executed in order to eliminate the threat of
dissidents. Among those labeled as dissidents were children,
church workers, and priests who would be kidnapped by the
authorities, tortured, and executed.

Nearing the liturgical remembrance of the passion and death
of Jesus, Romero recalls the suffering of the Salvadoran people,
the countless numbers of women, men, and children whose cries

---

3. Oscar Arnulfo Romero, "The Church in the Service of Personal, Community,
and Transcendent Liberation" (March 23, 1980). Full unedited text and audio of this
may be found at http://www.romerotrust.org.uk.

4. A reliable source for understanding the Christian tradition is the online Encyclopedia of the Dominican Order, NewAdvent.org. For understanding Holy Week and
Easter celebrations, please see http://www.newadvent.org/cathen/07435a.htm and
http://www.newadvent.org/cathen/05224d.htm, respectively.

for liberation reach out to God like the cries of the children of Israel in ancient Egypt. He states the names of victims, the dates on which they were attacked and murdered, the suffering that the "national security strategy" had left in its wake,[5] and he relates it to the biblical story of liberation *in history*. Reminding them of the liberation of the Israelites from the oppression of the Egyptians, Romero brought the poor and disenfranchised a message of hope for liberation *in history*. He spoke of his people as going through their own particular "exodus," and he spoke about a God who heard their cries in the same way the God of the Exodus heard those of the children of Israel.

Romero's stance throughout his leadership of the church in El Salvador was one of reconciliation. He understood that God's love encompasses all—victim and oppressor alike—desiring reconciliation and a new reality for all. The words in the second-to-last paragraph above are spoken directly to those who carry out orders to persecute and kill those suspected of dissent or those declared enemies of the state. Romero speaks with both judgment and hope for reconciliation, hope for a reality where the laying down of weapons is possible. He departs from the biblical narrative of Exodus here, expressing hope for the conversion of the hearts of Pharaoh and his army by asking the Salvadoran army to cease obeying unjust orders. He invites them to be part of the history of God's salvation, to join with God hearing the cries of the people. Romero does this by summoning divine authority to speak truth to power. The demand comes in his cry to lay down weapons. His message in this sermon appeals to soldiers by reminding them of their own condition of being oppressed by unjust structures and misguided leaders, and their shared destiny as Salvadorans.

---

5. To learn more about the way the national security strategy affected the civil war in El Salvador, please read "El Salvador: 12 Years of Civil War," from the Center for Justice and Accountability, http://www.cja.org/article.php?list=type&type=199.

Romero counts the soldiers among the poor, as brothers to the peasants, as one with the Salvadoran people. This speech represents his deepest appeal to their humanity and sense of justice, and therefore, the most dangerous message of his ministry.

Romero was assassinated on March 24, 1980, on orders given by members of the Salvadoran military. It is now public knowledge that some of the high-ranking military officials responsible for this murder, and those of other clergy during the twelve-year civil war, were trained at the School of the Americas in the United States, now known as the Western Hemisphere Institute for Security Cooperation.[6] Years later, Romero's sermons, poetry, and prayers remain as a witness of faithfulness to God in the face of terror. Romero's martyrdom—being killed as a result of hate of this faith—was recognized on January 2015, and his path to sainthood was confirmed at his beatification on May 23, 2015. San Romero de las Américas—Saint Romero of the Americas, as he has been known for the past few decades—is a reminder of the Christian call to be a presence for hope and transformation in history. His assassination marked a turning point for the church in Latin America and elsewhere, which up until then had been only tangentially involved in the political future of its people. It placed the church squarely on the side of the persecuted and suffering and made it an agent of reconciliation and peace. The final peace accords among the factions in El Salvador's cruel civil war were signed in 1992, brokered in part by the United Nations and leaders of the Catholic Church. The Salvadoran people had come to

---

6. The School of the Americas Watch is an organization that has dedicated itself to gathering information and maintaining protest and public pressure toward the closure of the School of the Americas. It aims to hold the United States military responsible for its role in fueling violence and terror in developing countries through the reinforcement of national security strategies, anti-dissident and counterinsurgency training of foreign officials, and weapons assistance to foreign governments involved in civil war, and sustains efforts to close down the SOA/WHISC. http://www.soaw.org/.

trust the role of the church in negotiating peace through the witness set by Romero and that of the clergy, women religious, and slain and abducted lay workers who followed and who paid a high price for their solidarity with the oppressed.

Christians are called to represent the person of Jesus in history. Romero is that figure who, within my lifetime, unequivocally witnessed to a Christ-like encounter with the suffering of the world. He is the example of a Christian completely enmeshed in the pain of his people, inviting me to do the same. Without a doubt, if one commits to the work of justice in a similar way, one is exposed to the pressures and persecution that followed Romero and others like him. This makes his witness easy to understand, but hard to follow. Can the contemporary Christian heart harness the empathic power to live into this radical vision of justice and peace? It is worth remembering that Romero himself struggled to grow into his role as a "voice for the voiceless," having begun his ministry as a rather bookish and sickly priest uninvolved in political matters. It was only through an intensive discernment process late in his life that he embraced his Moses moment and helped transform an entire nation.

Why, one might ask, have I chosen to share this text, written by a Catholic priest and addressed to an overwhelmingly Catholic audience, for an interfaith collection? There are a few reasons for my choice that are embedded in my presentation above, but which I want to make more explicit here. First, I think that Archbishop Romero's development into a prophetic leader, one who spoke out against injustice at great personal risk, is a model that transcends religious boundaries. Second, his message of peace *and* justice is one that I believe in deeply and want others within and beyond my faith community to consider. Romero cried out for an end to the violence and bloodshed that ravaged his country. In doing so, he sought to appeal to people's best selves, pleading with soldiers, freedom fighters, politicians, and peasants alike to remember their common humanity. Further, he urged all of his listeners—even the most sinful among them—to remember that despite their actions to date, if they made a genuine effort to change their ways, God still had a place for them in the divine kingdom. At the same time, he provided the oppressed with public pastoral support, insisting that their suffering was not in vain and that justice would prevail. While the imagery of the ancient Israelites or of Jesus may not speak to all readers, the messages of repentance and hope in the face of great pain and loss are widely applicable. Finally, Archbishop Romero "spoke truth to power" by insisting that there could be no genuine healing—no peace *or* justice—without an honest examination of the economic and political structures that supported widespread poverty and oppression throughout El Salvador. This call for systemic change remains a challenge to all people of faith and conscience throughout the world.

QUESTIONS FOR REFLECTION/DISCUSSION

1. Think of a moment in recent times when a religious leader (or leaders) in your community took a public stance for justice. What were the risks involved in doing so? What were the responses like?

2. What resources from your tradition would you draw from in order to speak boldly on a current justice issue? What elements might need to be adjusted for application in your context?

3. How do you respond to the story of Archbishop Romero? How might he serve as a resource for your own vision of justice and peace?

For Further Reading

"Archbishop Romero Assassination: CIA and Department of State Files." Compilation of declassified CIA and US State Department documents. Various dates. Available at http://www.paperlessarchives.com/archbishop-romero-cia-files.html.

Archbishop Romero Trust. http://www.romerotrust.org.uk/.

John Dear. "Romero's Resurrection." *National Catholic Reporter.* March 16, 2010. Available at http://ncronline.org/blogs/road-peace/romeros-resurrection.

Oscar Romero. *The Violence of Love.* Compiled and translated by James R. Brockman, SJ. San Francisco: Plough Publishing House, 1988.

Oscar Romero. *Voice of the Voiceless: The Four Pastoral Letters and Other Statements.* Maryknoll, NY: Orbis Books, 2001 (twelfth printing).

23

Clergy Beyond Borders

A Caravan of Reconciliation

AMY EILBERG

Early in the sabbatical year devoted to writing my book, *From Enemy to Friend: Jewish Wisdom and the Pursuit of Peace*, an irresistible opportunity came my way.[1] A dear colleague, Rabbi Gerry Serotta, had recently created Clergy Beyond Borders, an organization devoted to empowering religious leaders to promote interreligious understanding, as an expression of our shared, religiously grounded passion for peacebuilding. Gerry, whom I know to be a person of great integrity, courage, and good-heartedness, invited me to join in the organization's Caravan of Reconciliation, gathering clergy of three faiths to travel around the country together, beginning symbolically on September 11, 2011, to promote interreligious dialogue. I knew this invitation was a gift I should not refuse.

The caravan began in Washington, DC, setting out on a fifteen-day road trip traversing three thousand miles, addressing some five thousand people at university campuses, synagogues, churches, and Islamic centers in fifteen cities. Jewish, Christian, and Muslim clergy traveled in the caravan together, stopping for two or three

---

1. This essay is adapted from Rabbi Eilberg's book, *From Enemy to Friend: Jewish Wisdom and the Pursuit of Peace* (Maryknoll, NY: Orbis Books, 2014).

public events each day, where we offered teachings from our three traditions in support of active, respectful engagement with people of other religions. We spoke of the dangers to American democracy posed by rising trends of religious intolerance, particularly against American Muslims. We shared our own personal stories of passionate engagement between and among religious communities, and we offered prayers for peace in many languages.

Central to my experience of the caravan was the co-founder of Clergy Beyond Borders, Imam Yahya Hendi, the well-known and widely beloved Muslim chaplain at Georgetown University, the first Muslim ever to hold such a position on an American university campus. Brother Yahya (as he is affectionately known) is a force of nature, a person of boundless energy, enormous charisma, and a heart as loving as any I have known. Yahya, a Palestinian American, has a large sense of mission about this sacred work. He thinks boldly about possibilities for bringing people together across boundaries of religion and national origin. He was constantly planning how to promote our next engagement, how to engage more media, and how to expand the work throughout the country and around the world. Being in his presence evoked inspiration and hope.

The caravan experience was also defined by the loving friendship shared by Rabbi Gerry and Imam Yahya. Being in Gerry and Yahya's presence, one could not help but be moved by the love, admiration, and sheer inspiration that bound these two great religious leaders, working together for peace within and beyond their own religious communities. Their affection, respect, and deep sense of partnership with one another infused our experience.

Each morning, before setting off on the day's adventures, Yahya would sit in stillness for a moment in the driver's seat, then call us to prayer in our respective sacred languages. One morning I chanted the biblical words, "*Ma gadlu ma'asecha Yah,*" "How great are

Your works, O God, your thoughts are very deep" (Psalm 92:6), expressing my reverence for the beauty of this inspired group of people setting off for a day of sacred work, ready to travel many miles for the sake of peace. Pastor Steve Martin prayed spontaneously in the characteristic cadence of Evangelical Christians. In a tone both eloquent and conversational, he thanked God for the pleasures of friendship, camaraderie, and mutual appreciation in our relationships, and for the blessing of important work to fill our days. Finally, Yahya chanted the opening verses of the Qur'an:

> "*Bismillah...*"—"In the name of God, the Most Gracious, the Most Merciful. Praise be to Allah, Cherisher and Sustainer of the Worlds; Most Gracious, Most Merciful; Master of the Day of Judgment. It is You that we worship and Your help that we seek."[2]

These words have become dear to me, having so often heard Muslim colleagues begin meetings by calling us together into prayerful awareness with this text. The words and descriptions of God all have exact parallels in Hebrew, evoking in me a visceral sense of familial connection. The chant, beautiful and contemplative, filled our small van, consecrating our common space and time. It was sure to be a blessed day.

Each time the caravan rolled into another town and addressed another audience, I was asked to articulate the basis for positive interreligious engagement from within Jewish law and theology. Among the many texts I reached for was the following:

---

2. Holy Qur'an1:1. Translation adapted from Abdullah Yusuf Ali, ed., *The Meaning of the Holy Qur'an* (Beltsville, MD: Amana Publications, 1999).

Therefore, the human race was created from a single person, to teach that one who destroys one soul[3] is considered by Scripture as if he [or she] had destroyed an entire world; and whoever saves one soul is considered by Scripture as if he [or she] had saved an entire world. And for the sake of peace among people, that one should not say to his or her fellow, "My parent is greater than yours..." And to declare the greatness of the Holy One, blessed be God, for a human artisan stamps out many coins with one model and they are all alike, but the King, the King of kings, the Holy One, blessed be God, stamped each person with the seal of Adam, and not one of them is like his or her fellow. Therefore, each and every one is obliged to say, "For my sake the world was created." And lest you say, "What do we need with this trouble?" Has it not already been said, "He being a witness, whether he has seen or known, if he does not utter it, then he will bear his sin" (Leviticus 5:1).[4]

Always one of my favorite rabbinic texts, I especially love teaching this passage in the presence of Muslims. Since the first part of it also appears in the Qur'an, the text evokes a collective gasp of delight, one of those moments when we are reminded of the truth that Jews and Muslims are family, and that we revere sacred texts that express shared beliefs and values.

3. Many versions of this teaching say here "of Israel," suggesting that only Jewish lives are of ultimate value. I have long been convinced that the original mishnah, rich with universalistic creation imagery, must have intended to remind us of our kinship with all of humankind. I suspect that experiences of persecution led later Jewish editors to limit the scope of the mishnah's teaching. I recently learned that Professor Efraim E. Urbach has conclusively shown that "of Israel" is a later addition, not the original reading: *Tarbitz* 40 (5731): 268–84, with thanks to Professor David Golinkin for this reference.

4. Mishnah *Sanhedrin* 4:5.

In its original context in the Mishnah, this passage is a set of instructions given by judges to witnesses in capital trials. The witnesses are instructed sternly about the elemental value of every human life. They are to carry out their duties with rigorous honesty, purity of heart and intention, and reverence for the weightiness of their task. Nothing less than an infinitely valuable human life hangs in the balance.

This text, beloved by Jewish teachers both ancient and modern, is applied in many contexts in which the essential principle of human dignity is evoked,[5] and I can think of no more compelling rationale for the requirement to reach out to the religious other. The mishnah[6] offers four different aspects of the assertion that every human person is imbued with ultimate value.

1. The human race began with a single person. Evoking the story of creation, the mishnah recalls that in the beginning, one human person (Adam, followed by Eve) was the whole of the human race. As such, the destruction of any single person, from the perspective of creation, is equivalent to the destruction of all of humankind. It is a radical and challenging thought experiment for us, living in a world populated by some seven billion people, to imagine that the entire human race constitutes one—and then two—people. Yet this image brilliantly highlights the boundless

---

5. See, for example, Melissa Weintraub,"*Kvod Ha-Briot:* Human Dignity in Jewish Sources, Human Degradation in American Military Custody," T'ruah: The Rabbinic Call for Human Rights (formerly Rabbis for Human Rights–North America), http://www.truah/org. Rabbis Elliot N. Dorff, Daniel S. Nevins, and Avram I. Reisner, "Homosexuality, Human Dignity and Halakhah: A Combined Responsum for The Committee on Jewish Law and Standards," Rabbinical Assembly, http://www.rabbinical assembly.org.

6. A part of the Mishnah, a sixty-three-volume foundational work of Jewish law, compiled around 200 CE by Rabbi Judah the Prince, reflecting the first stage of Rabbinic law, including sources from several centuries of reflection in Rabbinic academies in Palestine.

value of every human life. From this perspective, the destruction of any human life is an earth-shattering catastrophe, and disrespect to any one person is itself a tragedy of global proportions.

2. We all descend from a single pair of ancestors. The mishnah traces all human lineage to a single pair of parents, Adam and Eve. This image suggests both an intimate kinship tie and complete equality of value among all human beings. The fact that we all descend from the same two parents means that we are literally members of the same family, back to the very beginning of time. Further, the fact of common lineage equalizes. No human being can claim descent more worthy than another's; no person can claim superiority to another by virtue of noble ancestry. We are all made of the same stuff, all the same at our core.

3. The miracle of human diversity. The mishnah lauds the Creator's wondrous act of creating the entire human race in the image of God. Unlike the human craftsman, whose copies of a single image are identical, each human person created in the image is inimitable and inestimably valuable. Every human person is imprinted with the seal of the first human being, sharing the characteristics that make us human, yet each of us is distinctive and irreplaceable.

The marvelous act of creation of humankind is a tribute to the Creator but also an indication of the incalculable worth of every person. Since each of us comes from the stock of Adam, we carry within us the DNA of the entire human race. The world was created for us, for all human beings throughout time. We are exhorted to know our own identity as the handiwork of the Holy One, the Creator of heaven and earth, the master Designer of all. The same is true of every member of the human family, without exception.

Further, the very appeal to creation imagery suggests a radical theology of diversity in the human family. To contemplate creation is to be filled with wonder at the stunning variety of beings in our world. We instinctively know that the wide range of creatures in the animal world is a beautiful thing. We know that a garden is far lovelier for the variety of species contained in it. Mountains and craters are more exquisite for the multifaceted impact of water and wind, affecting different areas differently, creating a spectacular array of colors, shapes, and forms.

The creation image reminds us as well that the fact that the other appears to be unlike me is not a mistake or an outrage. Why did God create people of different religions, ideologies, and national origins? Because God wanted the human race, like the floral world, to be a world of endless, exquisite diversity. The point is not to fight to force the other to become like me (as if that were possible). The challenge of human life is to be open to diversity as a gift, an invitation, an opportunity for mutual learning and enrichment.

4. Why bother? The instructions to the witnesses conclude with a penetrating challenge to human nature. The question "Why do we need this trouble?" originally addressed the fear, apathy, or laziness that might tempt witnesses to a crime to evade their responsibility to testify. The mishnah insists that sharing what one knows with the court for the sake of justice is a basic obligation of membership in society.

But we may apply the same question to the broader implications of this majestic sacred text. Why bother cultivating awareness of the infinite worth of every human life? Developing such consciousness is a lot of work, and acting on its implications even more so. To treat every person we meet as one entitled to the reverence due to the Creator imposes great demands on us. Couldn't we just forget, and succumb to the "natural" tendency to judge rather than extol the diversity of the human family?

The mishnah exhorts that maintaining such high standards of human dignity is a basic existential responsibility. The very nature of our existence mandates that we recognize the kinship and ultimate worth of all human beings, created just as we are, matchless and boundlessly precious. To fail to do so is to violate the very intention underlying our creation, and to dishonor the One who brought us to life.

As we all know, there are times when primal instincts lead us to violate these deepest human principles that lie at the heart of all interpersonal and intergroup relations. When the thinking mind is engaged, these immortal images and concepts have the power to help us override our baser instincts. Particularly in times of conflict and threat, we may need repeated reminders from holy texts and sacred community to return us to the commitments we hold most dear.

After a week on the caravan, my colleagues headed into Tennessee, where a debate raged about enacting "anti-shariah" legislation, prohibiting Muslims from following their own religious law, just as many Jews turn to *halacha* (Jewish law) to govern their religious lives. This was sure to be a challenging and fascinating leg of the trip, but it was time for me to go home to attend to other obligations.

It was bittersweet to leave my treasured friends and our sacred mission of peace education after many precious hours of shared love, laughter, and prayer. We had lived together for many days, on and off the van, creating for ourselves and modeling for others a world in which difference is not only tolerated but embraced and celebrated. Each of us had brought our whole self to the experience, including fierce loyalty to our own religious traditions, openness to exploring areas of strong disagreement, and delight in our common commitments. Most powerfully, we had been nourished by our shared mission to demonstrate the practice of honoring and caring for the religious other. Even in those moments when disagreement demanded difficult conversation, we had moved through it without compromising our compassion for one another.

It had been a joy and a privilege to participate. We had stimulated those we met along the way to commit to interreligious work in their own communities, and we had elicited many beautiful prayers for peace in many different languages on a sacred scroll that we took with us as we went on our way. I had tasted the rich blessing of living as one family across religious lines. I wish everyone could have such a blessed experience.

QUESTIONS FOR REFLECTION/DISCUSSION

1. What do you think causes the human instinct to fear those perceived as different? What might help us as a species to evolve to a place where embracing difference would come more naturally?

2. How do you connect a theology of creation with the work of engaging the religious other?

3. How do you understand the interplay of commonality and difference in the work of interreligious dialogue?

FOR FURTHER READING

Mary C. Boys. *Jewish-Christian Dialogue: One Woman's Experience*. Notre Dame, IN: Saint Mary's College, 1997.

Joan Chittister, Murshid Saadi Shakur Chishti, and Arthur Waskow. *The Tent of Abraham*. Boston: Beacon Press, 2006.

Diana Eck. *Encountering God: A Spiritual Journey from Bozeman to Banaras*. Boston: Beacon Press, 2003.

Eboo Patel. *Acts of Faith*. Boston: Beacon Press, 2007.

Jonathan Sacks. *The Dignity of Difference: How to Avoid the Clash of Civilizations*. London: Bloomsbury Academic, 2003.

Afterword

A Note on Interreligious Learning

Rabbi Daniel Lehmann
and Rev. Dr. Mary Elizabeth Moore

The contributors to this volume open worlds for the reader. As longtime interreligious learners, teachers, and scholars we have witnessed how such learning can open the spiritual and ethical worlds of the religious self and other. The study of religious texts is often a central aspect of religious life, and when we study texts with people from different traditions, we have the opportunity to explore some of our deepest commitments and questions. Interreligious learning requires becoming, in the words of Abraham, "a stranger and a resident" (Genesis 23:4) simultaneously.

The oscillation between acting as host and guest, between familiarity and strangeness, enables a richly textured relationship to grow from the soil of mutual learning. We become, in the language of the ancient rabbis, *havrutot*, study-mates and companions. The study partnership creates a bridge between religious cultures that enables us to cross into each other's spiritual homes as hospitable hosts and gracious guests. At the same time, it beckons us to offer respectful critique, to probe gently the inner life of our study partner in ways that reveal complexity, commonality, and difference. If this process is undertaken with care and sensitivity, a bond can grow between partners that is not easily broken, leading to interreligious friendships that dispel ignorance and displace prejudice. Such relationships, in turn, carry the seeds for communal and societal transformation as new possibilities for cooperative action emerge. The textual and interpersonal lessons of the *havruta* experience, including an appreciation for the universal *and* the particular, can serve to inspire new visions of interreligious living.

This book makes a distinctive and valuable contribution to the literature of interreligious learning and action, and we are grateful to all who contributed their knowledge, insights, and life experiences. Each chapter serves as a resource for study, contemplation, and discussion. Further, the contributors model for us how textual study can inspire various forms of interreligious engagement. We recommend that readers consider exploring these rich materials with a *havruta* partner, ideally from a different religious tradition, using the primary texts, interpretive essays, and guiding questions to reflect on their own religious and interreligious values and priorities. Echoing the sentiment of the editors in their introduction, we also recommend that you share with your study partner(s) texts from your tradition that inspire, guide, or authorize your participation in interreligious relationships.

Finally, we hope that scholars and educators will continue to build on this work, adding to the relatively small but growing body of literature on interreligious learning. The more experimentation that takes place in varied settings and through diverse modalities, the more we need to reflect on how interreligious study experiences can both deepen our particular identities and create greater connection and collaboration among people committed to different religious traditions.

Contributors

Esther Boyd is the manager of curriculum development at the Interfaith Youth Core (IFYC). She supports faculty working to develop courses and programs related to the emerging field of interfaith studies. She also manages the online curriculum Introduction to Interfaith Leadership and works on other IFYC academic initiatives programs. A humanist chaplain, Esther served at Johns Hopkins University for several years before joining the IFYC team. She is also an editor for the Humanist Chaplaincy thinkblog *Applied Sentience*. Esther holds an MA in religion and literature from Yale University.

Abigail Clauhs is a Unitarian Universalist chaplain, activist, and scholar. She is a graduate of Claremont School of Theology's Master of Divinity program in interfaith chaplaincy and is currently working as a hospital interfaith chaplain. Originally from South Carolina, Ms. Clauhs graduated summa cum laude with a BA from Boston University, where she majored in religion and minored in English. Ms. Clauhs became deeply involved in interfaith activism and social justice work in Boston, where she also began to discern a call to ministry. Currently a candidate for Unitarian Universalist fellowship and ordination, Ms. Clauhs continues to be involved in interfaith work and social justice organizing around racial justice, immigration, spiritual care, and other issues. She is also in process for Unitarian Universalist ordination.

Francis X. Clooney, SJ, is Parkman Professor of Divinity and professor of comparative theology at Harvard Divinity School. From 2010 to 2017, he was the director of the Center for the Study of

World Religions at Harvard. He is a leading figure globally in the developing field of comparative theology, a discipline distinguished by attentiveness to the dynamics of theological learning deepened through the study of traditions other than one's own. He has also written on the Jesuit missionary tradition, particularly in India, on the early Jesuit pan-Asian discourse on reincarnation, and on the dynamics of dialogue and interreligious learning in the contemporary world. He is a Roman Catholic priest and a member of the Society of Jesus, serving regularly in a Catholic parish on weekends.

MT Dávila is associate professor of Christian ethics at Andover Newton Theological School. Her scholarship focuses on the option for the poor, especially in the context of U.S. civil society. She has published in the areas of public theology, Latino/a ethics, the ethics of the use of force, the use of the social sciences in ethical reflection, racial justice, and immigration. She is currently working on a volume on the option for the poor in the United States as a key to transcending the culture wars.

Andrew R. Davis is assistant professor of Old Testament at Boston College School of Theology and Ministry with primary research interest in Israelite religion, especially sacred space. He studied classics at the University of North Carolina at Chapel Hill (AB). After a year in the Jesuit Volunteer Corps (Oakland) and another year teaching English in Austria, Davis attended the Weston Jesuit School of Theology (MTS) and then pursued doctoral studies at the Johns Hopkins University (MA, PhD). Research for his dissertation included a year as Kress Fellow at the Albright Institute of Archaeological Research in Jerusalem. Before coming to Boston College, Davis taught for four years at the Seattle University School of Theology and Ministry.

Amy Eilberg is the first woman ordained as a Conservative rabbi by the Jewish Theological Seminary of America. She serves as the director of the Pardes Rodef Shalom (Pursuer of Peace) Communities Program, helping synagogues and Jewish organizations place the pursuit of peace in interpersonal relationships at the center of their communal mission. Rabbi Eilberg also serves as a spiritual director and interfaith activist in the San Francisco Bay Area. Her book, *From Enemy to Friend: Jewish Wisdom and the Pursuit of Peace*, was published by Orbis Books in 2014. She received her doctor of ministry degree from United Theological Seminary of the Twin Cities in 2016.

Nancy Fuchs Kreimer is the founding director of the Department of Multifaith Studies and Initiatives at the Reconstructionist Rabbinical College where she is also associate professor of religious studies. She holds a master's degree from Yale Divinity School and a doctorate in religion from Temple University. She serves on the executive committee of Shoulder to Shoulder: Standing with American Muslims, Upholding American Values and is a founding board member of the Sisterhood of Salaam Shalom. Rabbi Dr. Fuchs Kreimer is the author of *Parenting as a Spiritual Journey* and co-editor of *Chapters of the Heart: Jewish Women Sharing the Torah of our Lives*.

Rahuldeep Gill, PhD, speaks and writes to inspire connected communities. He has spoken before diverse adult and student audiences of all sizes at events sponsored by the State Department's Study of United States Institutes, the Church Center for the United Nations, and the Interfaith Youth Core. The *Los Angeles Times*, Patheos.com, the Huffington Post, and LinkedIn have published his writings. His first book, *Drinking from Love's Cup*, was published by Oxford University Press. Dr. Gill is past director for the Center for Equality and Justice at California Lutheran University, where he is still a tenured faculty member and campus interfaith strategist. He is the visiting professor of Sikh Studies at the Graduate Theological Union in Berkeley. He has twice been voted Cal Lutheran's Diversity Professor of the Year and lives in Los Angeles with his family.

Ruben L. F. Habito, born in the Philippines, served as a Jesuit priest in Japan and taught for many years at Sophia University in Tokyo. Since 1989, he has taught at Perkins School of Theology, Southern Methodist University, where he is professor of world religions and spirituality and director of spiritual formation. He serves as guiding teacher of the Maria Kannon Zen community in Dallas, Texas, and continues to practice in the Catholic Christian tradition. He is the author of several books and articles, including *Healing Breath: Zen Spirituality for a Wounded Earth*; *Living Zen, Loving God*; and *Experiencing Buddhism: Ways of Wisdom and Compassion*. He has served as president of the Society for Buddhist-Christian Studies and is a member of the American Theological Society.

Soren M. Hessler is associate director of the Betty Ann Greenbaum Miller Center for Interreligious Learning & Leadership at Hebrew College and Chapel Associate for Leadership Development at Boston University's Marsh Chapel. He is an ordained elder in the West Ohio Annual Conference of the United Methodist Church and a member of the United Methodist Ecumenical and Interreligious Training Young Adult Network related to the ecumenical staff of the Council of Bishops. Reverend Hessler holds master's degrees in church administration, education, and theology from Boston University and is a practical theology PhD candidate at the university's school of theology, where his research focuses on the history and practice of accreditation at theological schools in the United States in the early twentieth century.

Celene Ibrahim is the Islamic studies scholar-in-residence at Hebrew College and Andover Newton Theological School. She has served as the Muslim chaplain for Tufts University since 2014 and is also an instructor at the Boston Islamic Seminary. Ms. Ibrahim has published widely on academic forums, and her contributions to increasing religious literacy have been featured in the *New York Times*, the Huffington Post, BBC Persian, Public Radio International, and the Religion Initiative of the Council on Foreign Relations, among other venues. A Harvard Presidential Scholar from 2008 to 2011, she is currently completing a doctorate in Arabic and Islamic civilizations at Brandeis University. Ms. Ibrahim holds an MA in women's and gender studies and Near Eastern and Judaic studies from Brandeis, an MDiv from Harvard Divinity School, and an AB in Near Eastern studies with highest honors from Princeton University.

Sherman A. Jackson is King Faisal Chair in Islamic Thought and Culture and Professor of Religion and American Studies and Ethnicity at the University of Southern California. Dr. Jackson's research interests focus on classical Islamic studies, including law, theology, and intellectual history, and extend to placing this legacy in conversation with the realities of modern Islam in the West, most especially Muslim communities in America. This implicates issues of race, immigration, liberalism, democracy, religion in the modern world, pluralism, constitutionalism, Muslim radicalism, and related areas of inquiry, all in conversation with the classical and post-classical legacies of Islam. He is at work on a major book, tentatively entitled: *Beyond Good and Evil: Shari'ah and the Challenge of the Islamic Secular.*

Daniel L. Lehmann is a Jewish innovator who has devoted his career to pluralistic Jewish education. In 2008, he became the eighth president of Hebrew College, where he also serves as professor of pluralism and Jewish education. Lehmann has rabbinical ordination from Yeshiva University, where he also received an undergraduate degree in philosophy. He has done graduate work in Jewish studies and education at both New York University and the Bernard Revel Graduate School of Yeshiva University and was a research fellow in Jewish education at Brandeis University. Prior to coming to Hebrew College, Lehmann served as the founding headmaster of Gann

Academy–The New Jewish High School of Greater Boston and was founding director of the Berkshire Institute for Music and Arts, now known as BIMA at Brandeis. He is passionately committed to inter-religious learning and leadership. Lehmann has been an active trustee of the Boston Theological Institute, most recently serving as chair of its board. He writes and lectures extensively on interreligious engagement as well as Jewish theology and education.

Timothy T. N. Lim, PhD, MDiv, BBA, is the incoming director of the Chinese Centre for Research and Training at Carey Baptist College, Auckland, New Zealand, and a visiting lecturer at the London School of Theology (London). Rev. Dr. Lim has published book chapters and peered-review articles on ecclesiology, ecumenism, evangelicalism, Pentecostalism, Reformed theology, theological interdisciplinarity, theology of culture, theology in Asia, and overcoming interreligious violence. He is author of *Ecclesial Recognition with Hegelian Philosophy, Social Psychology and Continental Political Theory* (2017).

Jeffery D. Long is professor of religion and Asian studies at Elizabethtown College in Elizabethtown, Pennsylvania, where he has taught since receiving his doctoral degree from the University of Chicago Divinity School in 2000. He is the author of *A Vision for Hinduism: Beyond Hindu Nationalism*, *Jainism: An Introduction*, and the *Historical Dictionary of Hinduism*, as well as numerous articles and public presentations. A central theme of his work is religious pluralism. He is currently writing an introductory textbook on Indian philosophy. Dr. Long practices Vedanta in the tradition of Sri Ramakrishna and Swami Vivekananda, in which he took initiation in 2005 from Swami Tyagananda.

Mahan Mirza, professor at the University of Notre Dame, is lead faculty in a project to advance scientific and theological literacy in madrasa discourses in India. He holds a BS in mechanical engineering from University of Texas, Austin; an M.A. from Hartford Seminary; and a PhD in religious studies from Yale University. He has taught a range of courses in Arabic-Islamic studies, Western religions, and history of science, along with foundational subjects in the liberal arts to undergraduates at Yale; California State University, Chico; Zaytuna College; and Notre Dame. He has edited two special issues of the *Muslim World* and served as assistant editor for the *Princeton Encyclopedia of Islamic Political Thought.* Dr. Mirza was previously at Zaytuna College for five years, serving as dean of faculty from 2013 to 2016.

Mary Elizabeth Moore is dean of the School of Theology and professor of theology and education at Boston University. Her passion is to journey with others to cultivate deeper faith, compassionate humanity, and a more just, peaceful, and sustainable world. An ordained United Methodist deacon, she feels privileged to work toward those ends with colleagues at Boston University and around the world, especially in the practices of knowing the Holy, building justice, resisting violence, and caring for the earth. Her books include *Teaching as a Sacramental Act*, *Ministering with the Earth*, *Covenant and Call*, *Teaching from the Heart*, and *The United Methodist Diaconate* (co-authored), plus three edited volumes. She has engaged in interreligious relationship-building in local, professional, and academic settings and is presently working on a project to develop interreligious approaches to practical theology.

Jennifer Howe Peace is associate professor of interfaith studies at Andover Newton Theological School and founding co-director of the Center for Interreligious and Communal Leadership Education (CIRCLE). Dr. Peace is a founding co-chair of the Interreligious and Interfaith Studies Program Unit of the American Academy of Religion, launched in 2013, and founder of the Association for Interreligious/

Interfaith Studies (AIIS), launched in 2017. Dr. Peace is the faculty consultant at Yale Divinity School for the Bridging Faith Traditions Program. In 2017, Dr. Peace was visiting associate professor of religious pluralism at Harvard Divinity School and a senior consultant to the Pluralism Project at Harvard. Author of numerous articles, essays, and chapters, Dr. Peace's latest book project is *Interreligious/Interfaith Studies: Defining a New Field*, co-edited with Eboo Patel and Noah Silverman (forthcoming from Beacon, 2018). She is the co-editor of *My Neighbor's Faith: Stories of Interreligious Encounter, Growth, and Transformation* (Orbis, 2012) and a series editor for *Interreligious Studies in Theory and Practice* for Palgrave Macmillan.

Anantanand Rambachan is professor of religion at St. Olaf College, Minnesota. He is also visiting professor at the Academy for the Study of World Religions at the University of Hamburg, Germany. His major books include: *Accomplishing the Accomplished: The Vedas as a Source of Valid Knowledge in Shankara*; *The Limits of Scripture: Vivekananda's Reinterpretation of the Authority of the Vedas*; *The Advaita Worldview: God, World, and Humanity*; and *A Hindu Theology of Liberation: Not-Two Is Not One*. The British Broadcasting Corporation broadcast a series of twenty-five of his lectures around the world.

Hussein Rashid, PhD, is founder of islamicate, L3C, a consultancy focusing on religious literacy and cultural competency. He works as a contingent faculty member. He has a BA in Middle Eastern studies from Columbia University, a masters in theological studies focusing on Islam, and an MA and PhD in Near Eastern languages and cultures focusing on South and Central Asia from Harvard University. His research focuses on Muslims and American popular culture. He writes and speaks about music, comics, movies, and the blogistan. He also has a deep interest in Shi'i justice theology. He is actively involved in numerous multi-faith activities in New York City.

Or N. Rose is the founding director of the Betty Ann Greenbaum Miller Center for Interreligious Learning & Leadership at Hebrew College. A prolific writer and editor, he is the creator of the weekly Jewish scriptural commentary "70 Faces of Torah" and, with Dr. Homayra Ziad, the interreligious series, "Can We Talk: A Jewish-Muslim Conversation," both of which appear on the Huffington Post. Rabbi Rose is also co-editor of several books, including *Jewish Mysticism & the Spiritual Life: Classical Texts, Contemporary Reflections* (Jewish Lights) and *My Neighbor's Faith: Stories of Interreligious Encounter, Growth, and Transformation* (Orbis). A founding faculty member of the Rabbinical School of Hebrew College, he speaks and teaches in academic, religious, and civic contexts throughout the United States on modern Jewish life and thought and interreligious and cross-cultural engagement.

Judith Simmer-Brown, PhD, is distinguished professor of contemplative and religious studies and has been a leader of interreligious dialogue and training at Naropa University since 1980. Acharya Simmer-Brown is on the board of the Society for Buddhist-Christian Studies and a frequent contributor to *Buddhist-Christian Studies*; she also serves as advisor to Monastic Interreligious Dialogue and is an advisory board member of *Dilitato Corde: Journal of Interreligious Dialogue Experience*. She was a member of the Cobb-Abe Theological Encounter from 1984 to 2004 and participated in the Gethsemane Dialogues in 1996 and 2002. She is co-author with Br. David Steindl-Rast and others of *Benedict's Dharma* and author of the preface to *Speaking of Silence*.

Simran Jeet Singh is an assistant professor in the Department of Religion at Trinity University. He is the senior religion fellow for the Sikh Coalition and the Henry R. Luce Post-Doctoral Fellow for Religion in International Affairs at NYU's Center for Religion and Media. Dr. Singh's academic expertise focuses on the history of religious communities and literatures in South Asia, and he also writes and speaks frequently on issues related to racial justice, interfaith relations, and hate violence in modern America. Dr. Singh holds a Ph.D. from Columbia University, a graduate degree from Harvard University, and an undergraduate degree from Trinity University.

Varun Soni is the dean of religious life at the University of Southern California, where he is also an adjunct professor in the School of Religion and a university fellow at the Center on Public Diplomacy. He holds degrees in religion from Tufts University, Harvard University, the University of California, Santa Barbara, and the University of Cape Town, as well as a law degree from the University of California, Los Angeles. He is the author of *Natural Mystics: The Prophetic Lives of Bob Marley and Nusrat Fateh Ali Khan*.

Joshua M. Z. Stanton is rabbi of East End Temple in Manhattan and a Senior Fellow of CLAL – The National Jewish Center for Learning and Leadership. In 2013, he was ordained from Hebrew Union College – Jewish Institute of Religion. He is a founding editor emeritus of the *Journal of Interreligious Studies*, a pioneering publication in the field of interreligious studies. He writes regularly for the Huffington Post and *Times of Israel*. Josh was one of just six finalists worldwide for the Coexist Prize and was additionally highlighted by the Coexist Forum as "one of the foremost Jewish and interreligious bloggers in the world." He serves as a trustee of the International Jewish Committee on Interreligious Consultations, which presides over Jewish-Christian relations with the Vatican and World Council of Churches.

Burton L. Visotzky is Appleman Professor of Midrash and Interreligious Studies at the Jewish Theological Seminary. There he serves as Louis Stein Director of the Finkelstein Institute for Religious and

Social Studies and directs the Milstein Center for Interreligious Dialogue. Rabbi Visotzky is the author of eleven books. The most recent, *Aphrodite and the Rabbis: How the Jews Adapted Roman Culture to Create Judaism as We Know It*, was published by St. Martin's Press in 2016.

Amos Yong is professor of theology and mission and director of the Center for Missiological Research at Fuller Theological Seminary in Pasadena, California. His graduate education includes degrees in theology, history, and religious studies from Western Evangelical Seminary (now George Fox Seminary), Portland State University, and Boston University and an undergraduate degree from Bethany University of the Assemblies of God. He has authored or edited more than forty volumes and is a member of the American Theological Society.

Homayra Ziad is a scholar-activist, educator, and writer with more than fifteen years' experience in religious and interreligious education and programming. After receiving a doctorate in Islamic Studies from Yale, she was assistant professor of Islam at Trinity College and currently leads the integration of Islam and Muslim communities at the Institute for Islamic, Christian, and Jewish Studies (ICJS) in Baltimore. At ICJS, she creates programs for activists and emerging religious leaders to explore the intersection of religion and social justice. She speaks regularly to raise public awareness of Islam and Islamophobia and serves on the board of the American Civil Liberties Union (ACLU) of Maryland. Homayra is also co-chair of the American Academy of Religion's Interreligious and Interfaith Studies Group. She has written for many academic and popular venues and consults for the media. The heart of her work lies in Islamic spirituality, creative religious expression through the arts and humor, and the struggle for religious and racial equity.

Index

al-Abidin, Zayn, 162–63
Acts II, narrative of, 42, 43–44,
    44–46, 46–51
Ali, 159–67, 168
American Jewish Committee (AJC),
    130–32, 134–36
Archangel *Jibrīl,* 82–83, 167
Arjan, Guru, 148, 153–54, 192
Arlington Street Church, 33–34
Aurangabadi, Siraj, 104, 105–6,
    108–9

Babur, 191–94, 195, 196
Bamba, Amadou, 163–64
Bea, Augustin, 130–36
Bhagavad Gita, 173, 175, 178
Boyle, Gregory, 79
Buddha, 3–11, 12

Caravan of Reconciliation. *See*
    Clergy Beyond Borders
Cathedral of the World concept,
    31–35, 38–39, 40–41
chosenness, concept of, 53–61
Church, Forrest, 31, 34, 35, 38–39,
    40, 41
Clergy Beyond Borders, 219–27

Dei Verbum (Word of God), 129–30,
    133
The Dignity of Difference (Sacks),
    58–59

Eck, Diana, 125
Eisen, Arnold, 61
Ekam sat text. *See* R̥g Veda
El Salvador, 209–10, 212–17

Elazar bar Shimon, Rabbi, 66–70, 71
Evangelicals, 48, 74, 221

Faruqi, Abdul Wahab (Sachal
    Sarmast), 104–5, 107–8
Francis, Pope, *xi, xii*
free will, 24, 197, 199

Gabriel, Archangel, 82–83, 167
Gandhi, Mohandas K., 17, 18–19,
    171, 177
Gautama, Siddhartha, 3–11, 12
al-Ghazali, 28
Gitagovinda (poem), 115–16
Green, Arthur, 59, 61, 62, 124
Grossman, David, 121–22, 124, 125,
    126, 127
Guru Granth Sahib, 148, 191,
    195–96

havruta (peer study), 121–22,
    124–25, 126, 229–30
Hebrew Bible, 65, 124, 134, 197
Hemingway, Ernest, 29
Hendi, Yahya, 220–21
hermeneutic of love, 75, 80
Heschel, Abraham Joshua, 130–36,
    137, 200–7
Hindu ideal, Vivekananda
    expounding, 171, 172–78
hukam (God's will), 197
Humanist Manifesto III, 94–95

Imam Ali, 159–67, 168
Imam Jafar, 163, 165
interreligious dialogue
    19th century view of, 170

AJC experience, 130–31, 131–37
Caravan of Reconciliation,
promoting, 219
divergence as a possible
outcome, 50
ego, keeping out of dialogue,
126–27
questions for reflection, 29, 51,
207, 227
as a sacred practice, 124–25
Vatican II documents as
inspiring, 129, 181–82
interreligious engagement
Clergy Beyond Borders, 219–27
consensus, holding off from, 90
goals and methods, *xvi,* 84–85
interreligious friendship, 46–51,
230
in Jewish practice, 54, 221–23
Muslim perception of, 144
Nostra Aetate as encouraging,
188
prayer *vs.* panels, 86
qawwali, as characterizing, 110
questions for reflection, 48, 50,
51, 80, 199
"Sanso Ki Maalam," interfaith
spirit of, 113–19
in Sikhism, 149, 151, 153
as transformative, 40

Jewish-Catholic relations, 129–37
John XXIII, Pope, 130, 180

Kalama-Sutta (Discourse to the
Kalamas), 3–11
Kaplan, Mordecai, 53–56, 57, 60
Kennedy, John F., 200–1, 204, 207
Khan, Aga, 165
Khan, Daulat, 192
Khan, Nusrat Fateh Ali, 113–14,
117–19
Khan, Shah Rukh, 113
Khusrau, Amir, 103

King, Martin Luther, Jr., 203, 204–6
King, Thomas Starr, 35
Krishna, 105, 108, 112, 115–16, 117

Lazarus, Emma, 93–94, 96, 99
Lubac, Henri de, 185

makhloket (debate), 121, 123–24,
126
Martin, Steve, 221
Mishnah, 68, 133, 135, 223–26
Mormons, Shabbat experience of,
121, 122–24
Muhammad, Prophet
Archangel *Jibrīl* and, 82–83, 167
as defamed, 87
faith in the Messenger, 23
in *The Family of 'Imrān,* 141–42
grandchildren, possessing *nur,*
159–60
as guided, 27
intercessory powers of, 161–62
Medina, move to, 140–41
as a mercy to humankind, 88
praise poems in honor of, 104
as relatable, 164–65
in *viraha* tradition, 115, 116
Muridiyya, veneration of, 163–64

Nanak, Guru, 148–52, 191–99
Nayyar, Adam, 116–17
"The New Colossus" (poem), 93–94,
96
Niebuhr, Reinhold, 140, 206
Nostra Aetate (In Our Time),
129–30, 133–34, 137,
181–89, 206

"On the Rosary of my Breath." *See*
"Sanso Ki Maala"
Otto, Rudolf, 39

Parliament of the World's Religions,
170–71, 172–73, 176

Paul VI, Pope, 180
Pentecostals, 47, 48
People of the Book, 140, 141–43
predestination, 24, 27

qawwali music, 103–4, 106, 107,
    110, 114, 118
Qur'an
    on diversity as a test, 25–26
    God, describing, 88–89, 164
    on good and evil deeds, 146
    historical claims, 145, 147
    Imam, on the concept of, 161,
        165
    on the Jews, 140, 141–43, 145
    music and, 106–7
    non-linear nature of text, 144
    on predisposition, 27
    Sūra 64 on faith, 23–24
    Sūrah al-'Alaq, 82–83, 83–88

Radha, 115–16
Radical Judaism (Green), 59
Rahman, A. R., 117–18
Rahner, Karl, 185
Ramdas, Guru, 148, 152–53
Reconstructionists, 53, 54–57
Ṛg Veda, 13–14, 14–21
Romero, Oscar, 209–11, 211–13,
    213–17
Rumi, Jalaluddin, 163

Sachal Sarmast, 104–5, 107–8
Sacks, Jonathan, 58
as-Sadiq, Jafar, 163, 165

"Sanso Ki Maala," 112, 113–19
Sells, Michael, 23
Selma march, 35, 204–5, 207
Serotta, Gerry, 219–20
Shimon bar Yohai, Rabbi, 66
Shuster, Zachariah, 130, 131–32
Sohila, recitation of, 148, 149–54
Statue of Liberty, 93–94, 99
Stendahl, Krister, 58, 61
Sufi Comics, 168
Sufis, on the journey towards God,
    108–9
Sūrah al-'Alaq verses, 82–83,
    83–88
Synoptic Gospels, 72–80

Talib, Ali ibn Abi, 159–67, 168
Talmud, 65–69, 126
TaNaKh (Hebrew Bible), 65, 124,
    134, 197
Tannenbaum, Marc, 132
theodicy, 197, 199
theology of creation, 47, 227
Tusi, Nasir un-Din, 164
Twain, Mark, 113

Unitarian Universalist theology. *See*
    Cathedral of the World
    concept

Vatican II, 129–30, 180–81, 202,
    206, 211
viraha poetic tradition, 115
Vivekananda, Swami, 171, 172–78,
    178–79